Mary Sue Taylor

Prayer for Daybreak and Day's End

VOLUME I

January Through June

St.
ANTHONY
MESSENGER
PRESS

CINCINNATI, OHIO

In gratitude to

Father Inocencio Estibalez
and
Father Edward Lamp

for their spiritual direction
and inspiration

Nihil Obstat: Rev. Thomas Richstatter, O.F.M.
Rev. Robert L. Hagedorn

Imprimi Potest: Rev. John Bok, O.F.M.
Provincial

Imprimatur: Rev. R. Daniel Conlon, V.G.
Archdiocese of Cincinnati
July 19, 1993

The *nihil obstat* and *imprimatur* are a declaration that a book is considered to be free from doctrinal or moral error. It is not implied that those who have granted the *nihil obstat* and *imprimatur* agree with the contents, opinions or statements expressed.

Scripture citations are taken from *The New American Bible With Revised New Testament,* copyright ©1986 by the Confraternity of Christian Doctrine, and are used by permission. All rights reserved.

Cover and book design by Julie Lonneman
Illustrations by Paula Wiggins

ISBN 0-86716-147-7

Published by St. Anthony Messenger Press
Printed in the U.S.A.

Introduction

Rising early, you stumble, still sleepy-eyed, to your place of prayer. At day's end, you refuse the welcoming bed while you weave the day's loose ends into your prayer. Such moments put you in community with the priests, religious and laity all over the world who celebrate common prayer at fixed intervals throughout the day.

The Liturgy of the Hours (also referred to as the Divine Office or the Breviary) has its origins in Christ himself, who enjoined us to "pray unceasingly." From the times of the early Church, believers have gathered at specified times, day and night, to pray and praise God. United in prayer, the community of the faithful lifts its collective voice in psalmody and joins with Christ and the Church in a prayer for all of humankind—especially at the "hinges" of the day, morning and evening.

This easy-to-use book of Morning and Evening Prayers borrows from the tradition. While the Liturgy of the Hours is a voluminous, complex and costly four-volume set, this two-volume set offers a simplified, concise format. It is arranged by date. Volume One begins with New Year's Day and ends with June 30; Volume Two will take you from July 1 to December 31. All you need to do is turn to the day's date. The Canticles, one of which closes each prayer session, are printed on a separate card that will serve as your bookmark.

The Components of Morning Prayer

Morning Prayer begins with a salutation and continues with a selection from Psalms. These Opening Songs are used for an entire week. (The fourth "week" of each month has more than seven days.)

Scripture Reading: Most of the Scripture selections follow the Church's liturgical calendar; others relate to the season or to a particular theme. Scripture passages are kept short purposely. You are invited to read the surrounding text in your own Bible, so that the meaning is understood in its proper context.

Because dates for Lent and Easter vary each year, this calendar-based book does not include prayer for specific seasonal days (Ash Wednesday, Good Friday, etc.). Prayers for February and March, however, follow a Lenten theme while prayers for April focus on the Resurrection.

Putting Prayer Into Practice gives suggestions for integrating the Scripture into daily life. *Words of Wisdom* come from a spiritual master, usually a saint, pope or theologian. A *Meditation* or *Spiritual Exercise* is a discipline to expand and deepen the soul's prayer journey. Only one of these techniques is used each day; they are presented alternately throughout the book.

Prayer: A gentle prayer-poem builds on the Scripture theme and sets the mood for carrying spiritual values into the day's work and play.

Canticle: One of the beautiful word-songs attributed to saints and biblical figures and found on the bookmark.

The Components of Evening Prayer

Evening Prayer begins with a salutation and continues with a selection from Psalms. These Opening Songs are used for an entire week. (The fourth "week" of each month has more than seven days.)

Scripture Reading: The Scripture selection for Evening

Prayer is usually the same as for Morning Prayer.

Reflection: A few questions upon which to reflect, based on the Scripture theme and the practical suggestions for applying the Scripture theme to daily life. Suggestions for keeping a spiritual journal are given occasionally.

Prayer: A brief prayer of thanksgiving or praise.

Canticle: Another of the word-songs found on the bookmark.

Overall, this book attempts to present a prayer expression geared for the spirituality of the 1990's and beyond. May it enrich your prayer life!

January

Opening Song for Morning Prayer

SALUTATION

Morning Light,
first of the new year:
I salute the Creator
of such radiance.

SONG Psalm 84:1-6

How lovely is your dwelling place,
    O LORD of hosts!
My soul yearns and pines
    for the courts of the LORD.
My heart and my flesh
    cry out for the living God.
Even the sparrow finds a home,
    and the swallow a nest
    in which she puts her young—
Your altars, O LORD of hosts,
    my king and my God!

Happy they who dwell in your house!
    continually they praise you.
Happy the men whose strength you are!
    their hearts are set upon pilgrimage....

*Turn to the page with today's date for the continuation of
Morning Prayer.*

Opening Song for Evening Prayer

SALUTATION

Gently may the sun smile
as it sets on our efforts at new beginnings.

SONG Psalm 84:9-12

O LORD of hosts, hear my prayer;
  Hearken, O God of Jacob!
O God, behold our shield,
  and look upon the face of your anointed.
I had rather one day in your courts
  than a thousand elsewhere;
I had rather lie at the threshold of the house of my God
  than dwell in the tents of the wicked.
For a sun and a shield is the LORD God;
  grace and glory he bestows.
The LORD withholds no good thing
  from those who walk in sincerity.
O LORD of hosts,
  happy the men who trust in you!

*Turn to the page with today's date for the continuation of
Evening Prayer.*

Morning Prayer

Begin with page 6.

SCRIPTURE Galatians 4:4-7

> But when the fullness of time had come, God sent his
> Son, born of a woman, born under the law, to ransom
> those under the law, so that we might receive adoption.
> As proof that you are children, God sent the spirit of his
> Son into our hearts, crying out, "Abba, Father!" So you
> are no longer a slave but a child, and if a child then also
> an heir, through God.

MEDITATION EXERCISE

> On this day of new beginnings, explore in your heart
> what Paul means by the words, "You are no longer a
> slave but a child, and if a child then also an heir through
> God." What kingdom or inheritance are you an heir to?
> How are you going to go about claiming your
> inheritance?

> As you start the new year, move, think and act with the
> knowledge and confidence of your personal riches.

PRAYER

> I am the child of a King
> and my riches,
> though neither silver nor gold,
> bring joy and peace.
> Come, Christ,
> and make your kingdom
> here in my heart.

CANTICLE Canticle of Mary

Evening Prayer

Begin with page 7.

SCRIPTURE Galatians 4:7

> So you are no longer a slave but a child, and if a child
> then also an heir, through God.

REFLECTION

> Do I think of myself as rich?

PRAYER

> King of Love,
> You supply me with all that I need.
> For the riches of your wisdom and love,
> bountiful God, I am grateful.

CANTICLE Wisdom Canticle

Morning Prayer

Begin with page 6.

SCRIPTURE 1 John 2:24-27

Let what you heard from the beginning remain in you. If what you heard from the beginning remains in you, then you will remain in the Son and in the Father. And this is the promise that he made us: eternal life. I write you these things about those who would deceive you. As for you, the anointing that you received from him remains in you, so that you do not need anyone to teach you. But his anointing teaches you about everything and is true and not false; just as it taught you, remain in him.

MEDITATION

Many of the spiritual masters, even psychologists, theorize that within each one of us lies the ultimate truth or knowledge of all things. We have only to strip away the layers of ego, selfishness, passion, illusion, and so on to get to this core of truth. Meditate on how you can become more honest with yourself and others.

PRAYER

It is easy for me to see, Lord, that as long as I have a passion for anything, even an idea or a way of doing things, I am not free to see the truth.

CANTICLE Wisdom Canticle

Evening Prayer

Begin with page 7.

SCRIPTURE *See page 10.*

REFLECTION

How am I set in my ways? In what situations do I block the truth?

PRAYER

For the truth you give us
and the power it brings,
I thank you, Creator God,
Alpha and Omega:
for truth that is not overtaken
by the lure of the world,
truth that disdains power, wealth and fame—
seeking, instead, a heart of integrity!

CANTICLE Canticle of Zechariah

Morning Prayer

Begin with page 6.

SCRIPTURE 1 John 2:15-17

Do not love the world or the things of the world. If
anyone loves the world, the love of the father is not in
him. For all that is in the world, sensual lust, enticement
for the eyes, and a pretentious life, is not from the Father
but is from the world. Yet the world and its enticement
are passing away. But whoever does the will of God
remains forever.

SPIRITUAL JOURNAL

A spiritual journal is a diary of your spiritual life—a log of
what is happening to you internally. If you would like to
keep one, buy a little book with blank pages and begin to
record your spiritual insights, thoughts, practices, even
dreams. It is not necessary to make an entry every day.
(Throughout this book there will be suggestions for
entries in your spiritual journal.)

Today's Scripture reading provides a good incentive to
develop the spiritual, eternal part of your being. Meditate
on God's will for you and enter it in your journal. Date all
entries.

PRAYER

Give me a sensible spirit, loving God,
One which is not overtaken by the lure of the world
One that disdains power, wealth and fame
And seeks, instead, a heart of integrity!

CANTICLE Canticle of St. Patrick

Evening Prayer

Begin with page 7.

SCRIPTURE *See page 12.*

REFLECTION

Do I have trouble discerning God's will for me? What steps can I take that will bring me closer to knowing God's will for me?

PRAYER

Gentle, loving God,
you are always there,
drawing us to you.
With a grateful heart,
I embrace you.

CANTICLE Canticle of Judith

Morning Prayer

Begin with page 6.

SCRIPTURE John 1:14

And the Word became flesh
and made his dwelling among us,
and we saw his glory,
the glory as of the Father's only Son,
full of grace and truth.

PUTTING PRAYER INTO PRACTICE

How can you give flesh to your words? Try today to put
your words into action. If you wish for something, do one
deed that will bring you closer to realizing that wish. If
you criticize something, find a way to make a difference
regarding the problem you criticize. Remember that
most accomplishments are won one small step at a time.

PRAYER

I am the indwelling Christ,
present within you.
I am he who was first;
long ago you were with me.
Awake from your sleep of forgetfulness
and you will know
I was always there.

CANTICLE Wisdom Canticle

Evening Prayer

Begin with page 7.

SCRIPTURE *See page 14.*

REFLECTION

In what ways today did I put my words into action?

PRAYER

You have filled my life
with grace and truth.
How wonderful is your dwelling place,
Father, Son and Holy Spirit.

Glory be to the Father....

CANTICLE Canticle of Zechariah

Morning Prayer

Begin with page 6.

SCRIPTURE 1 John 4:16b

God is love, and whoever remains in love remains in God and God in him.

WORDS OF WISDOM

The three stages to union with God are purification, illumination and union. The spiritual journey is, in a sense, an effort of concentration. In his *Spiritual Canticle* St. John of the Cross describes the concentration of union:

All the powers of the soul together, because of the union in the inner cellar, drink of the Beloved.... This draught of God's most deep wisdom makes the soul forget all the things of this world, and consider all its previous knowledge, and the knowledge of the whole world besides, as pure ignorance in comparison with this knowledge.

Go back over the Scripture readings for January 2, 3 and 4. See how they all come together in the wisdom of the Spirit.

PRAYER

Take this cup and drink deeply.
I alone am the draught that slakes your thirst.
I am the Living Water,
the Wine of Life.

CANTICLE Wisdom Canticle

Evening Prayer

Begin with page 7.

SCRIPTURE *See page 16.*

REFLECTION

What concentrated effort can I make each day to abide in love? Did I make any of those efforts today? How?

PRAYER

Beloved, let me drink of
the cup of your love
and be present to the times
when you offer it.

CANTICLE Canticle of St. Francis

Morning Prayer

Begin with page 6.

SCRIPTURE Exodus 20:2-6

I, the LORD, am your God, who brought you out of the land of Egypt, that place of slavery. You shall not have other gods besides me. You shall not carve idols for yourselves in the shape of anything in the sky above or on the earth below or in the waters beneath the earth; you shall not bow down before them or worship them. For I, the LORD, your God, am a jealous God, inflicting punishment for their fathers' wickedness on the children of those who hate me, down to the third and fourth generation; but bestowing mercy down to the thousandth generation, on the children of those who love me and keep my commandments.

COMMENTARY

There is a temptation among many to turn God into an abstraction—a cold, impersonal force. Even our use of inclusive language tends to foster the idea of God as an "it" or a machine, rather than a loving, living consciousness. It is only when we see God as a compassionate, fiery, vibrant being that we are willing to make commitments, sacrifice, even die, in order to flow with the spirit of this divine presence.

PRAYER

> You give me the ability
> to see you in your glory, God.
> I pray that I take the time
> to respond to that ability.

> Glory be to the Father....

CANTICLE Canticle of Mary

Evening Prayer

Begin with page 7.

SCRIPTURE *See page 18.*

REFLECTION

> How much do I dare to allow the vibrant, loving presence
> of God to enter my being?

PRAYER

> I dance in joy at the thought
> of your mercy and love for me.
> Hallelujah!

CANTICLE Canticle of Judith

Morning Prayer

Begin with page 6.

SCRIPTURE Matthew 2:1b-3, 7-12

...[M]agi from the east arrived in Jerusalem, saying "Where is the newborn king of the Jews? We saw his star at its rising and have come to do him homage." When King Herod heard this, he was greatly troubled, and all Jerusalem with him.... Then Herod called the magi secretly and ascertained from them the time of the star's appearance. He sent them to Bethlehem and said, "Go and search diligently for the child. When you have found him, bring me word, that I too may go and do him homage." After their audience with the king they set out. And behold, the star that they had seen at its rising preceded them, until it came and stopped over the place where the child was. They were overjoyed at seeing the star, and on entering the house they saw the child with Mary his mother. They prostrated themselves and did him homage. Then they opened their treasures and offered him gifts of gold, frankincense, and myrrh. And having been warned in a dream not to return to Herod, they departed for their country by another way.

PUTTING PRAYER INTO PRACTICE

Christ brings light into our lives. Usually it is not a bright, illuminating flash but a slow, steady, enlightening glow. When convenient, rise early before the sky shows any light. Sit outdoors or by a window and watch the daybreak. The first streak of light is exciting. Minute by minute it grows lighter. It happens so gradually that you will not be able to perceive a change. But you know it is happening because within an hour or so the sun is shining all around you. God is like the sun in our lives—always there shining even when we don't notice it.

PRAYER

Light of the World, come:
cast out the darkness within me.

CANTICLE Canticle of St. Patrick

Evening Prayer

Begin with page 7.

SCRIPTURE *See page 20.*

REFLECTION

What clouds in my life block the sun (the Son) from shining down on me?

PRAYER

For your warmth, light and healing rays,
Brother Sun, Sister Moon,
Son of God,
I praise and thank you.

CANTICLE Canticle of St. Francis

Opening Song for Morning Prayer

SALUTATION Isaiah 60:1

Rise up in splendor! Your light has come,
the glory of the Lord shines upon you.

SONG Psalm 72:1-7

O God, with your judgment endow the king,
and with your justice, the king's son;
He shall govern your people with justice
and your afflicted ones with judgment.
The mountains shall yield peace for the people,
and the hills justice.
He shall defend the afflicted among the people,
save the children of the poor,
and crush the oppressor.

May he endure as long as the sun,
and like the moon through all generations.
He shall be like rain coming down on the meadow,
like showers watering the earth.
Justice shall flower in his days,
and profound peace, till the moon be no more.

*Turn to the page with today's date for the continuation of
Morning Prayer.*

Opening Song for Evening Prayer

SALUTATION Isaiah 60:2

> See, darkness covers the earth,
> > and thick clouds cover the peoples;
>
> But upon you the LORD shines
> > and over you appears his glory.

SONG Psalm 72:16-19

> May there be an abundance of grain upon the earth;
> > on the tops of the mountains the crops shall rustle like
> > > Lebanon;
> >
> > the city dwellers shall flourish like the verdure of the
> > > fields.
>
> May his name be blessed forever;
> > as long as the sun his name shall remain.
>
> In him shall all the tribes of the earth be blessed;
> > all the nations shall proclaim his happiness.

> Blessed be the LORD, the God of Israel,
> > who alone does wondrous deeds.
>
> And blessed forever be his glorious name;
> > may the whole earth be filled with his glory. Amen.
> > Amen.

Turn to the page with today's date for the continuation of Evening Prayer.

Morning Prayer

Begin with page 22.

SCRIPTURE Matthew 2:13b-15, 19-20

...[B]ehold, the angel of the Lord appeared to Joseph in a dream and said, "Rise, take the child and his mother, flee to Egypt, and stay there until I tell you. Herod is going to search for the child to destroy him." Joseph rose and took the child and his mother by night and departed for Egypt. He stayed there until the death of Herod, that what the Lord had said through the prophet might be fulfilled, "Out of Egypt I called my son."

...When Herod had died, behold, the angel of the Lord appeared in a dream to Joseph in Egypt and said, "Rise, take the child and his mother and go to the land of Israel, for those who sought the child's life are dead."

PUTTING PRAYER INTO PRACTICE

Think of a time when a dream had a special significance for you and, because of the dream's message, you altered your plans.

PRAYER

Let me die a little, Lord,
to my ways of doing things,
so that I may always be ready and alert
to alter my course for you.

CANTICLE Canticle of Judith

Evening Prayer

Begin with page 23.

SCRIPTURE *See page 24.*

REFLECTION

Am I too possessive of my own ways of dealing with a slight, an affront to my dignity, an injustice? Do I want to cling to the sadness of these things rather than drop them and continue my journey without burden and care?

PRAYER

For the ability to drop the past
and sail into the future unencumbered,
I thank you, Lord.

CANTICLE Wisdom Canticle

Morning Prayer

Begin with page 22.

SCRIPTURE Luke 2:41-43, 46-49

Each year [Jesus'] parents went to Jerusalem for the feast of Passover, and when he was twelve years old, they went up according to festival custom. After they had completed its days, as they were returning, the boy Jesus remained behind in Jerusalem, but his parents did not know it.... After three days they found him in the temple, sitting in the midst of the teachers, listening to them and asking them questions, and all who heard him were astounded at his understanding and his answers. When his parents saw him, they were astonished, and his mother said to him, "Son, why have you done this to us? Your father and I have been looking for you with great anxiety." And he said to them, "Why were you looking for me? Did you not know that I must be in my Father's house?"

PRAYER

Enable me, Divine Light
as I grow in gifts and grace,
to be about your business more and more
and to remain undisturbed
by the lure of the world's business.

CANTICLE Canticle of St. Patrick

Evening Prayer

Begin with page 23.

SCRIPTURE *See page 26.*

REFLECTION

In what ways was I about God's business today?

PRAYER

God, you are a patient and protective provider.
May I grow in your likeness
and be ever grateful for your providence.

CANTICLE Canticle of Mary

Morning Prayer

Begin with page 22.

SCRIPTURE Matthew 3:13-17

Then Jesus came from Galilee to John at the Jordan to be baptized by him. John tried to prevent him, saying, "I need to be baptized by you, and yet you are coming to me?" Jesus said to him in reply, "Allow it now, for thus it is fitting for us to fulfill all righteousness." Then he allowed him. After Jesus was baptized, he came up from the water and behold, the heavens were opened [for him], and he saw the Spirit of God descending like a dove [and] coming upon him. And a voice came from the heavens, saying, "This is my beloved Son, with whom I am well-pleased."

PUTTING PRAYER INTO PRACTICE

With his baptism, Jesus began his public ministry. It was a small step for him but what overwhelming implications for humankind! Pleasing his father carried him to glory and persecution, freedom of the spirit and the suffering of the cross, death and resurrection. Are you prepared to allow those extremes in your life to please God? Be honest with yourself and honest with God as you tell him what you are prepared to allow in your life.

PRAYER

> Prepare me, Lord,
> for the path you wish me to take.
> Help me to understand
> that allowing your will to unfold in my life
> is what gives it meaning.

CANTICLE Canticle of Zechariah

Evening Prayer

Begin with page 23.

SCRIPTURE *See page 28.*

REFLECTION

> Did I tell God, honestly, the ways I will allow him to work
> in my life? Did I tell him where to keep his hands off?

*Enter your reflections in your spiritual journal, if you are
keeping one.*

PRAYER

> For allowing yourself to be an instrument of my
> salvation, I thank you, Brother Jesus.

CANTICLE Wisdom Canticle

Morning Prayer

Begin with page 22.

SCRIPTURE John 1:35-39a

The next day John was there again with two of his
disciples, and as he watched Jesus walk by, he said,
"Behold, the Lamb of God." The two disciples heard
what he said and followed Jesus. Jesus turned and saw
them following him and said to them, "What are you
looking for?" They said to him, "Rabbi" (which translated
means Teacher), "where are you staying?" He said to
them, "Come and you will see."

PUTTING PRAYER INTO PRACTICE

In your spiritual journey, what are *you* looking for? Ask
yourself that question today when you are engaged in an
activity that does not require great concentration—such
as waiting in line, flossing your teeth, cleaning a closet.
Ask that question of a few people you are close to. This is
a wonderful way to find God, together.

PRAYER

What I look for in you,
Lamb of God,
depends on what curve I'm going around
or which road I'm taking
in my own spiritual journey.
How rich to share with fellow travelers
the tales of my soul's quest
and to hear in turn
about their search for you.

CANTICLE Canticle of Zechariah

Evening Prayer

Begin with page 23.

SCRIPTURE John 1:39

He said to them, "Come, and you will see."

REFLECTION

In what ways did I imitate Christ today?

PRAYER

For your invitation to me to "come and see," I am
grateful, Lamb of God.

CANTICLE Canticle of Mary

Morning Prayer

Begin with page 22.

SCRIPTURE John 1:12-13

...[T]o those who did accept him he gave power to become children of God, to those who believe in his name, who were born not by natural generation nor by human choice nor by a man's decision but of God.

PUTTING PRAYER INTO PRACTICE

A birth is holy because the soul is sent by God. With a holy birth, the soul comes to earth alive with the memory of its divine mission. Awaken that memory within you! Do not think that Jesus or John the Baptist are the only holy births. To those who accept Christ, he gave power to become children of God. Following your own ideals, tastes and interests is not the way to discover your divine mission. When you awaken your memory of home—home with the Father—you will discover your Father's will for you. This awakening comes with a struggle—a struggle between the sleep of illusion (pleasures of the temporal life) and wakefulness to the Christ-consciousness within you.

PRAYER

Awaken, my soul,
to the memory of home,
the union with the blessed, divine Essence.

CANTICLE Canticle of St. Patrick

Evening Prayer

Begin with page 23.

SCRIPTURE *See page 32.*

REFLECTION

Did I discover, even in a small way, a little more about
my Father's will for me?

PRAYER

For my divine home
and royal parentage,
give me a grateful heart,
Lord and God.

CANTICLE Canticle of Judith

Morning Prayer

Begin with page 22.

SCRIPTURE Wisdom 18:14-15a

For when peaceful stillness compassed everything
   and the night in its swift course was half spent,
Your all-powerful word from heaven's royal throne
   bounded, a fierce warrior, into the doomed land....

WORDS OF WISDOM

Wherever God the Father declares his Word within
the soul, wherever the place of this birth may be, and
wherever the soul may be receptive to this event, this
must be in the purest and most noble and most tender
place that the soul can offer.... For this reason the soul
in which the birth is to take place must remain very
pure and must live in a way that is very noble and very
collected and very spiritual. This soul must not flow
out through the five senses into the multiplicity of
creatures. It must rather remain quite inward and
collected and in its purest state....

The Father generates his Son in the true unity of
the divine nature. Behold, in the *same* and no other
way God the Father generates his Son in the
foundation *of the soul* and in its being, and he thus
unites himself with the soul. (Meister Eckhart)[1]

PRAYER

> Help me to reach that pure and tender place
> where your word gives birth
> to the divine nature
> in my soul.

CANTICLE Canticle of Judith

Evening Prayer

Begin with page 23.

SCRIPTURE *See page 34.*

REFLECTION

> Rest in gratitude and awe of the divine possibilities
> within your soul.

PRAYER

> I am overwhelmed, Lord,
> at the thought of union with you.
> Although I am not worthy,
> I give thanks for your abundant blessings.

CANTICLE Wisdom Canticle

Morning Prayer

Begin with page 22.

SCRIPTURE John 3:8

The wind blows where it wills, and you can hear the sound it makes, but you do not know where it comes from or where it goes; so it is with everyone who is born of the Spirit.

PUTTING PRAYER INTO PRACTICE

No one knows the ways of the Lord or the Spirit that comes from on high. The "Spirit within us" is a mystery. To be a receptacle for this Spirit or to recognize it in yourself or others involves setting aside self-complacency and rigid ideas of God.

Today, try to learn one good thing from each person you meet. Accomplish this by pinpointing a positive quality in everyone and imitating it.

PRAYER

O silence,
intoxicate me with your sound
so that I may be carried
to that secret place in my heart
and hear the Spirit sing its own song.

CANTICLE Wisdom Canticle

Evening Prayer

Begin with page 23.

SCRIPTURE *See page 36.*

REFLECTION

In what ways did I recognize the Spirit in other people today?

PRAYER

For sharing your Spirit,
Creator God,
I sing in thanksgiving.

Glory be to the Father....

CANTICLE Canticle of Judith

Opening Song for Morning Prayer

SALUTATION

> Prince of Light,
> I hear you call me
> out of darkness into your illuminating presence.

SONG Psalm 62:2-3, 6

> Only in God is my soul at rest;
>   from him comes my salvation.
> He only is my rock and my salvation,
>   my stronghold; I shall not be disturbed at all....
>
> Only in God be at rest, my soul,
>   for from him comes my hope.

Turn to the page with today's date for the continuation of Morning Prayer.

Opening Song for Evening Prayer

SALUTATION

Sister Moon,
you are God's gift to earth.
We delight in your ever-changing image,
your reflection of light.

SONG Psalm 62:6-8

Only in God be at rest, my soul,
　　for from him comes my hope.
He only is my rock and my salvation,
　　my stronghold; I shall not be disturbed.
With God is my safety and my glory,
　　he is the rock of my strength; my refuge is in God.
Trust in him at all times, O my people!
　　Pour out your hearts before him;
　　God is our refuge!

Turn to the page with today's date for the continuation of Evening Prayer.

Morning Prayer

Begin with page 38.

SCRIPTURE 1 Samuel 3:8-10

The LORD called Samuel again for the third time. Getting up and going to Eli, he said, "Here I am, You called me." Then Eli understood that the LORD was calling the youth. So he said to Samuel, "Go to sleep, and if you are called, reply, 'Speak, LORD, for your servant is listening.'" When Samuel went to sleep in his place, the LORD came and revealed his presence, calling out as before, "Samuel, Samuel!" Samuel answered, "Speak, for your servant is listening."

SPIRITUAL EXERCISE

To be God's servant in the world and to do God's bidding is to be content with the knowledge that all you do is a gift to the Spirit and from the Spirit. Truly, work becomes play and sacrifice becomes joy. Rest in this thought for a few minutes.

PRAYER

Give me the ears and the daring, God,
to hear you call and to say,
"Speak, Lord, your servant is listening,"
so that I may grow in my efforts
to put your will into action in my life.

CANTICLE Wisdom Canticle

Evening Prayer

Begin with page 39.

SCRIPTURE *See page 40.*

REFLECTION

Think back on the day. At which times were you filled
with joy and peace—even though things may not have
been running smoothly? At what times were you
anxious? What do these emotions say to you?

PRAYER

For your word
which refreshes
and brings new life,
I thank you, Creator God.

CANTICLE Canticle of Mary

Morning Prayer

Begin with page 38.

SCRIPTURE Mark 2:23-28

As [Jesus] was passing through a field of grain on the
sabbath, his disciples began to make a path while picking
the heads of grain. At this the Pharisees said to him,
"Look, why are they doing what is unlawful on the
sabbath?" He said to them, "Have you never read what
David did when he went into the house of God when his
companions were hungry? How he went into the house
of God when Abiathar was high priest and ate the bread
of offering that only the priests could lawfully eat, and
shared it with his companions?" Then he said to them,
"The sabbath was made for man, not man for the
sabbath. That is why the Son of Man is lord even of the
sabbath."

SPIRITUAL EXERCISE

To find out who you are, set some time aside and make a
deliberate effort to stop the everyday world from
encroaching. The more you are able to stop the inner
dialogue and return to the Source of your being, the
sooner you will discover who you are. The very risk of
self-discovery is threatening. But until you run the risk of
confronting yourself, you will not run the risk of
confronting God.

Take fifteen minutes to sit in silence; stop your thoughts.
Some sacred music may help move you into the spiritual
realm. If you are distracted by your worries or thoughts,

say the Our Father slowly, over and over, concentrating on each word. If your mind wanders, start the prayer again. If you choose this as a daily discipline, you will go far in developing spiritual maturity.

PRAYER

Lead me, Lord,
into the leisure of self-forgetfulness,
where I will not only find you
but also myself.

CANTICLE Canticle of Mary

Evening Prayer

Begin with page 39.

SCRIPTURE *See page 42.*

REFLECTION Did I dare to turn off the world of distractions and face myself today?

PRAYER

Lord of the Sabbath,
you give me everything I need.
Thank you for your divine blessing.

CANTICLE Canticle of Zechariah

Morning Prayer

Begin with page 38.

SCRIPTURE 2 Corinthians 5:17

So, whoever is in Christ is a new creation; the old things have passed away; behold, new things have come.

PUTTING PRAYER INTO PRACTICE

Christ shows us the power of love and light. When you make choices based on love rather than personal gain, the selfishness of your old self gives way to a new, higher light.

Pay attention to your decisions today. Notice which ones are based on love and which ones are based on self-interest.

PRAYER

At the beginning of this new year,
Spirit of Life,
give me the power and courage to change,
to throw off my old selfish ways
and to choose the path of light and love.

CANTICLE Canticle of St. Patrick

Evening Prayer

Begin with page 39.

SCRIPTURE *See page 44.*

REFLECTION

Which decisions did I make today based on love for others? What emotions and feelings surrounded these choices?

Enter your reflections in your spiritual journal, if you are keeping one.

PRAYER

Brother Jesus,
you came to give me
the power of love and light.

CANTICLE Canticle of St. Francis

Morning Prayer

Begin with page 38.

SCRIPTURE Luke 4:16-19

[Jesus] came to Nazareth, where he had grown up, and went according to his custom into the synagogue on the sabbath day. He stood up to read and was handed a scroll of the prophet Isaiah. He unrolled the scroll and found the passage where it was written:

"The Spirit of the Lord is upon me,
   because he has anointed me
      to bring glad tidings to the poor.
He has sent me to proclaim liberty to the captives
   and recovery of sight to the blind,
      to let the oppressed go free,
and to proclaim a year acceptable to the Lord."

PUTTING PRAYER INTO PRACTICE

The word *Christ* means "anointed one." Through baptism, you are anointed and bathed in the spirit of the Lord. Today, reflect on the needs around you and your own gifts. How is the Lord calling you to serve him?

PRAYER

> God of Freedom,
> Spirit of Service,
> lead me out of bondage.
> Free me from my own compulsions,
> mind-sets and passions
> so that I may be
> at liberty to serve others.

CANTICLE Canticle of St. Patrick

Evening Prayer

Begin with page 39.

SCRIPTURE *See page 46.*

REFLECTION

> To what am I in bondage?

PRAYER

> You give meaning and direction to my life,
> Divine Creator.
> I am indeed blessed!

CANTICLE Canticle of Judith

Morning Prayer

Begin with page 38.

SCRIPTURE Mark 3:13

[Jesus] went up to the mountain and summoned those whom he wanted and they came to him. He appointed twelve [whom he also named apostles] that they might be with him and he might send them forth to preach....

PUTTING PRAYER INTO PRACTICE

When it was time for Jesus to make one of the most important decisions in his life, he went to the mountain to pray and discern the Father's will. Do this today and every day when you have choices to make. You won't always have time to go to the mountain, but you will have some time for silence and prayer.

PRAYER Act of Consecration

I vow and consecrate to God all that is in me:
my memory and my actions to the Father;
my understanding and my words to the Son;
my will and my thoughts to the Holy Spirit;
my heart, my body, my tongue, my senses and all my
    sorrows
to the sacred humanity of Jesus Christ,
who was content to be betrayed into the hands of wicked
    men
and to suffer the torment of the cross. (Francis de Sales)

CANTICLE Wisdom Canticle

Evening Prayer

Begin with page 39.

SCRIPTURE *See page 48.*

REFLECTION

What will be my way of "going up to the mountain" and
how can I incorporate this habit into my life?

*Enter your reflections in your spiritual journal, if you are
keeping one.*

PRAYER

For giving me your love,
your strength and your spirit,
Brother Jesus,
whenever I go to the mountain.
I am overwhelmed by your compassion!

CANTICLE Canticle of Mary

Morning Prayer

Begin with page 38.

SCRIPTURE Proverbs 27:7

> One who is full, tramples on virgin honey;
>> but to the man who is hungry, any bitter thing is sweet.

MEDITATION

Prosperity does not bring satisfaction but the desire for more. Poverty, on the other hand, leads a person to grasp at anything. Simplicity, then, appears to be the key.

Meditate on the ways you can simplify your life and share your excess of time and goods with those living in poverty.

PRAYER

Awaken in me the artist,
Creator God.
Teach me the art of living simply
so that others
may simply live.

CANTICLE Canticle of Mary

Evening Prayer

Begin with page 39.

SCRIPTURE *See page 50.*

REFLECTION

Did I make an effort to simplify my life today? How do I feel about the excess I have? Is God calling me to share more with others?

PRAYER

Your life was a statement in simplicity,
Brother Jesus.
Thank you for helping me
cut through the complexities of living.

CANTICLE Canticle of St. Francis

Morning Prayer

Begin with page 38.

SCRIPTURE Isaiah 9:1

The people who walked in darkness
  have seen a great light;
Upon those who dwelt in the land of gloom
  a light has shone.

PUTTING PRAYER INTO PRACTICE

Where there is excess, there is usually addiction. And
where there is addiction, there is darkness. Look at the
excesses in your life again today. Look for the more
subtle habits that take you away from reality—that keep
you from becoming the best you can be: "addictions" to
soap operas, romance novels, sexual fantasies, worrying,
daydreaming, overscheduling, overworking. Even prayer
and religion can be overdone.

PRAYER

Lord, help me focus
on living the moment
and being alive in relationship
to myself, you and others.

CANTICLE Wisdom Canticle

Evening Prayer

Begin with page 39.

SCRIPTURE Isaiah 9:1

Upon those who dwelt in the land of gloom,
a light has shone.

REFLECTION

Am I willing to deal with one "addiction" in my life and to
try to uncover the pain that it is hiding?

PRAYER

For bringing me out of the darkness
and rescuing me from the gloom of the pit,
I thank you,
God of Light.

CANTICLE Canticle of Judith

Opening Song for Morning Prayer

SALUTATION

Lord,
you are the Fountain of Life.
May your divine grace
overflow in my heart.

SONG Psalm 104:1-6

Bless the LORD, O my soul!
   O LORD my God, you are great indeed!
You are clothed with majesty and glory,
   robed in light as with a cloak.
You have spread out the heavens like a tent-cloth;
   you have constructed your palace upon the waters.
You make the clouds your chariot;
   you travel on the wings of the wind.
You make the winds your messengers,
   and flaming fire your ministers.
You fixed the earth on its foundation,
   not to be moved forever;
With the ocean, as with a garment, you covered it;
   above the mountains the waters stood.

Turn to the page with today's date for the continuation of Morning Prayer.

Opening Song for Evening Prayer

SALUTATION

As the day closes,
I wrap the cloak of night about me
and seek the one whom my heart loves.

SONG Psalm 104:31-35

May the glory of the LORD endure forever;
    may the LORD be glad in his works!
He who looks upon the earth, and it trembles;
    who touches the mountains, and they smoke!
I will sing to the LORD all my life;
    I will sing praise to my God while I live.
Pleasing to him be my theme;
    I will be glad in the LORD.
May sinners cease from the earth,
    and the wicked be no more.
Bless the LORD, O my soul! Alleluia.

Turn to the page with today's date for the continuation of Evening Prayer.

Morning Prayer

Begin with page 54.

SCRIPTURE Psalm 104:1, 3c

Bless the LORD, O my soul!
O LORD, my God, you are great indeed!

PUTTING PRAYER INTO PRACTICE

Walk in a park today. Hear the music of the Spirit issuing
from the breeze as it brushes leaves and limbs. Take
pleasure in a branch glistening in the sun or powdered
with snow. Feel the Spirit of God close to you as it travels
on the wings of the wind. God is all around you. Breathe
in God's divine presence.

PRAYER

Deliver me, Divine Spirit,
from the machine,
from the cement.
Help me to remember
the place in the trees
where you and I meet.

CANTICLE Wisdom Canticle

Evening Prayer

Begin with page 55.

SCRIPTURE *See page 56.*

REFLECTION

Do I take time to get in touch with the earth, to soar with the spirit of the wind?

PRAYER

For beauty
both seen and unseen,
I thank you, Creator God.

CANTICLE Canticle of St. Francis

Morning Prayer

Begin with page 54.

SCRIPTURE John 13:34

I give you a new commandment: love one another. As I
have loved you, so you should also love one another.

WORDS OF WISDOM

God was pregnant with every creature from all eternity
so that all creatures might enjoy with him his goodness.
And among all these creatures, he does not love any one
more than any other. For insofar as creatures are open to
receive him, to that extent God pours himself out into
them.... God poured his being in equal measure to all
creatures, to each as much as it can receive. This is a
good lesson for us that we should love all creatures
equally with everything which we have received from
God. If some are naturally closer to us through
relationship or friendship, we should nonetheless
respond from divine love with equal friendliness to all
because we see all in relationship to that ultimate good
which is God. (Meister Eckhart)[2]

PRAYER

Divine Creator,
it is I who hold myself back from you.
Give me the daring to spread my arms wider
and open my heart more fully
so that you may fill it with your love
and I may empty it out again to those around me.

CANTICLE Canticle of St. Patrick

Evening Prayer

Begin with page 55.

SCRIPTURE *See page 58.*

REFLECTION

I am a vessel of God's light and love. What can I do to
enlarge the capacity of my vessel?

PRAYER

For all that you give me
and all that you are waiting to give me,
I give thanks, Lord.

CANTICLE Wisdom Canticle

Morning Prayer

Begin with page 54.

SCRIPTURE Hebrews 10:36; 10:7

Behold, I come to do your will, O God.

PUTTING PRAYER INTO PRACTICE

You need endurance to do the will of God and receive
what God has promised. Generally, you know what God
wants of you because of what has been revealed through
the Scriptures. Meditate on what God wants of you in
terms of relationship. How can you be more loving with
those closest to you?

PRAYER

Even in my generosity, Lord,
I often give to feel good;
I give what I desire to give
rather than what the other needs.
Give me the grace to be genuine, God,
in loving my brother and sister.

CANTICLE Canticle of St. Patrick

Evening Prayer

Begin with page 55.

SCRIPTURE *See page 60.*

REFLECTION

How much self-interest is there in my love for those people with whom I have intimate relationships?

PRAYER

You give me all I need to fulfill your will.
You carry me when I fall;
you pour down your gifts on me—
although sometimes I'm too busy to notice.
You give me a love that is pure.

Glory be to the Father....

CANTICLE Canticle of Mary

Morning Prayer

Begin with page 54.

SCRIPTURE James 4:8

Draw near to God, and he will draw near to you.

CENTERING PRAYER

This prayer tradition stems from the Jesus Prayer, or Prayer of the Heart, used for centuries by people who wanted to deepen their prayer life.

Pick a word that expresses your love for the divine, such as *God, Jesus, Love, Light, Abba, Father, Hosannah.* Pick a word that is significant to you. It could be a foreign word or no word at all—just a syllable or two. The purpose of this word is to center you in your union with the divine. Spend the day thinking about your choice of a prayer word. Tomorrow you will put it into practice.

PRAYER

Favor me, God,
in my return to the center,
which is you,
the source of life.

CANTICLE Wisdom Canticle

Evening Prayer

Begin with page 55.

SCRIPTURE James 4:8

Draw near to God, and he will draw near to you.

REFLECTION

What special word will draw me near to God?

PRAYER

You are the center of the universe,
Faithful Yahweh.

CANTICLE Canticle of Judith

Morning Prayer

Begin with page 54.

SCRIPTURE James 4:8

Draw near to God, and he will draw near to you.

CENTERING PRAYER *(continued from January 25):*

Sit in a relaxed position with your back straight. Close
your eyes and say the Our Father slowly. Slow your
breathing as much as possible. When you finish the Our
Father, take up your prayer word and say it over and over
in rhythm with your breathing. Whenever it feels right,
let go of the word and rest in the presence of the Lord,
who is the center of your being. When you are
distracted, take up your prayer word again to help you
return to the center.

When you come out of prayer, end with the Our Father.
Since it takes most people several minutes to unwind and
get into a proper prayer posture, this prayer requires a
minimum of five to ten minutes. As you get comfortable
with the silence and stillness, extend the time to suit
your own prayer pace.

CANTICLE Canticle of St. Francis

Evening Prayer

Begin with page 55.

SCRIPTURE James 4:8

Draw near to God, and he will draw near to you.

CENTERING PRAYER

Practice the Centering Prayer again. It is a wonderfully simple way to get in touch with the divine presence within you. At the close, pray in thanksgiving for God's touch.

CANTICLE Wisdom Canticle

Morning Prayer

Begin with page 54.

SCRIPTURE Mark 4:25

To the one who has, more will be given; from the one who has not, even what he has will be taken away.

COMMENTARY

The heart which has a close relationship with God will benefit more and more from the fruits of grace as it opens itself up to God's abundance. The heart which has not yet made the divine connection, however, will lose whatever little blessing it had to start with.

PRAYER

You are the vine and I am the branch, O God.
Do not allow me to cut myself off from you,
for surely my soul would wither and die.

CANTICLE Wisdom Canticle

Evening Prayer

Begin with page 55.

SCRIPTURE *See page 66.*

REFLECTION

Do I see myself as being the one who "has"? If so, am I appreciative and grateful for what I have?

PRAYER

I am your child, Creator God.
You lavish me with love and attention.
Even in my difficulties, you teach and console me.
Lucky am I to be known by you.

CANTICLE Canticle of Mary

Morning Prayer

Begin with page 54.

SCRIPTURE Mark 4:37-41

A violent squall came up and waves were breaking over the boat, so that it was already filling up. Jesus was in the stern, asleep on a cushion. The disciples woke him and said to him, "Teacher, do you not care that we are perishing?" He woke up, rebuked the wind, and said to the sea, "Quiet! Be still!" The wind ceased and there was great calm. Then he asked them, "Why are you terrified? Do you not yet have faith?" They were filled with great awe and said to one another, "Who then is this whom even wind and sea obey?"

PUTTING PRAYER INTO PRACTICE

When there is chaos and crisis around you, do not give in to it. Make decisions based on faith. You do not have to work for the emergency squad to be surrounded with chaos. Offices where people work for a paycheck rather than service or accomplishment are in chaos; families where members are each looking out for number one are in chaos. Resist the temptation to give in to the mentality of disorder and go along with the crowd.

PRAYER

Allow me, Prince of Peace,
to restore and maintain calm
in the midst of the chaos
of selfishness pride, ego and fear.

With your strength and direction,
order and harmony can prevail.

CANTICLE Canticle of St. Patrick

Evening Prayer

Begin with page 55.

SCRIPTURE *See page 68.*

REFLECTION

In what ways did I restore calm to a chaotic situation
today?

PRAYER

Thank you, Brother Jesus,
for calming my nerves,
comforting me when I am fearful
and giving me hope in times of crisis.

CANTICLE Canticle of Zechariah

Morning Prayer

Begin with page 54.

SCRIPTURE Hebrews 10:16b

I will put my laws in their hearts,
and I will write them upon their minds.

PUTTING PRAYER INTO PRACTICE

Heart is just as important for the trash collector as it is
for the clergy. The mason laying a brick wall with heart
brings more to the wall than just brick, mortar and
technique. Heart is loving what you do rather than doing
what you love. Such an attitude frees you for happiness
every moment rather than imprisoning you in the
have-to-do. Today, strive to put your heart into every
situation.

PRAYER

Let me look at things in a new way, Lord,
so that I may treat each task, each problem
as a precious opportunity sent by divine providence.
May I put my heart, my attention,
into each moment that the Spirit of Life offers.

CANTICLE Canticle of St. Patrick

Evening Prayer

Begin with page 55.

SCRIPTURE *See page 70.*

REFLECTION

At what times today was I bored and distracted? Why?

PRAYER

Your laws, Lord,
point the path to fulfillment.
Thank you for the lessons life brings.

CANTICLE Wisdom Canticle

Morning Prayer

Begin with page 54.

SCRIPTURE John 9:39

...I came into this world for judgment, so that those who do not see might see, and those who do see might become blind.

WORDS OF WISDOM

I hear and behold God in every object yet understand God not in the least. (Walt Whitman)

PRAYER

Elusive and mysterious Spirit,
Mother, Father, Brother, Child,
you whom my heart knows
but my mind cannot conceive:
Teach me your ways
as my soul flies into infinity.

CANTICLE Canticle of St. Patrick

Evening Prayer

Begin with page 55.

SCRIPTURE *See page 72.*

REFLECTION

Where did you see God today?

PRAYER

Even in my pride and stubbornness
you pour out your love and understanding
I close my eyes in gratefulness,
Compassionate Creator!

CANTICLE Canticle of Mary

Morning Prayer

Begin with page 54.

SCRIPTURE Luke 12:35-37

Gird your loins and light your lamps and be like servants who await their master's return from a wedding, ready to open immediately when he comes and knocks. Blessed are those servants whom the master finds vigilant on his arrival.

COMMENTARY

According to Meister Eckhart, reason and will are part of the soul, not the body. Too often the eyes of our body are preoccupied with the world of the senses and the eyes of the soul's reason and will are not vigilant or attentive to the world of the spirit.

PRAYER

Awake, my soul, and gaze at your God.
Do not sleep in the world of the senses
for spirituality is waiting on the Lord.

CANTICLE Wisdom Canticle

Evening Prayer

Begin with page 55.

SCRIPTURE Luke 12:37

Blessed are those servants whom the master finds vigilant on his arrival.

REFLECTION

To what things in life am I attentive and what things do I ignore?

PRAYER

Brother Jesus,
you brought me a new way of thinking,
a choice between waking up or remaining asleep.
Thank you for that freedom of choice.

CANTICLE Canticle of Zechariah

Notes

[1] Excerpt from *Breakthrough: Meister Eckhart's Creation Spirituality*, copyright ©1980 by Matthew Fox, is used by permission of Image Books, Doubleday & Co.

[2] Excerpt from *Breakthrough: Meister Eckhart's Creation Spirituality*, copyright ©1980 by Matthew Fox, is used by permission of Image Books, Doubleday & Co.

February

Opening Song for Morning Prayer

SALUTATION

Just as the dark night of the soul
leads to union with the beloved,
so too will the bleak, wintry days
lead to the spring of new life.

SONG Psalm 34:2-9a

I will bless the LORD at all times;
   his praise shall be ever in my mouth.
Let my soul glory in the LORD;
   the lowly will hear me and be glad.
Glorify the LORD with me,
   let us together extol his name.

I sought the LORD, and he answered me
   and delivered me from all my fears.
Look to him that you may be radiant with joy,
   and your faces may not blush with shame.
When the afflicted man called out, the LORD heard,
   and from all his distress he saved him.
The angel of the LORD encamps
   around those who fear him, and delivers them.
Taste and see how good the LORD is....

Turn to the page with today's date for the continuation of Morning Prayer.

Opening Song for Evening Prayer

SALUTATION

May my heart burn for God's justice
and my hands toil to ward off oppression.

SONG Psalm 34:16-21

The LORD has eyes for the just,
   and ears for their cry.
The LORD confronts the evildoers,
   to destroy remembrance of them from the earth.
When the just cry out, the LORD hears them,
   and from all their distress he rescues them.
The LORD is close to the brokenhearted;
   and those who are crushed in spirit he saves.
Many are the troubles of the just man,
   but out of them all LORD delivers him;
He watches over all his bones;
   not one of them shall be broken.

Turn to the page with today's date for the continuation of Evening Prayer.

Morning Prayer

Begin with page 78.

SCRIPTURE Mark 6:7-11

[Jesus] summoned the Twelve and began to send them
out two by two and gave them authority over unclean
spirits. He instructed them to take nothing for the
journey but a walking stick—no food, no sack, no money
in their belts. They were, however, to wear sandals but
not a second tunic. He said to them, "Wherever you enter
a house, stay there until you leave from there. Whatever
place does not welcome you or listen to you, leave there
and shake the dust off your feet in testimony against
them."

PUTTING PRAYER INTO PRACTICE

Cut out one thing today that is cluttering up your ability
to respond to God's word in your life. This "thing" could
be an attitude, a habit or a possession.

PRAYER

Give me the stamina to simplify my life, Lord.
Help me to realize I have only one need
and that is the need to love.

Evening Prayer

Begin with page 79.

SCRIPTURE *See page 80.*

REFLECTION

Does Jesus's message to the Twelve have anything to do with his message to me?

PRAYER

Thank you, Lord, for teaching me
that my happiness
is not dependent on a person or a thing.
My happiness depends on nothing else
but my willingness to love.

CANTICLE Canticle of Saint Francis

Morning Prayer

Begin with page 78.

SCRIPTURE Luke 2:30

...[M]y eyes have seen your salvation,...

PUTTING PRAYER INTO PRACTICE

God loved Simeon so much that he would not let him die before seeing the Son. Even today God reveals the Son to us in different places and faces. It is a disturbing thought, but Jesus is especially present in the poor. Remember that when you see a mother with many unkempt children or an unshaven street person.

PRAYER

Son of God,
because you choose humility and simplicity
I will find you now
among the humble and the meek.

CANTICLE Canticle of Zechariah

Evening Prayer

Begin with page 79.

SCRIPTURE Luke 2:30

...[M]y eyes have seen your salvation,...

REFLECTION

Did I find God today in at least one needy person?

PRAYER

Thank you, Creator God,
for all you have revealed
and continue to reveal to me. Amen.

CANTICLE Canticle of Mary

Morning Prayer

Begin with page 78.

SCRIPTURE James 3:5b-8

Consider how small a fire can set a huge forest ablaze.
The tongue is also a fire. It exists among our members as
a world of malice, defiling the whole body and setting the
entire course of our lives on fire, itself set on fire by
Gehenna. For every kind of beast and bird, of reptile and
sea creature, can be tamed and has been tamed by the
human species, but no human being can tame the
tongue. It is a restless evil, full of deadly poison.

PUTTING PRAYER INTO PRACTICE

When you speak today, remember that you are speaking
in God's presence. Before you answer the phone, invite
the Holy Spirit to put words into your mouth.

PRAYER

St. Blase,
protect my tongue and throat
from disease and poison.
May my voice and my words
echo honesty and forgiveness.

CANTICLE Canticle of St. Patrick

Evening Prayer

Begin with page 79.

SCRIPTURE John 1:1

In the beginning was the Word,
and the Word was with God,
and the Word was God.

REFLECTION

If someone recorded all of my conversations today,
would I be ashamed of any parts of the recording?

PRAYER

I dance, laugh and sing in your presence, Lord.
You have given me the ability
to communicate and express myself.
May my expression grow in purity and clarity.

CANTICLE Canticle of Zechariah

Morning Prayer

Begin with page 78.

SCRIPTURE Matthew 8:20b

...Foxes have dens and birds of the sky have nests, but the Son of Man has nowhere to rest his head.

PUTTING PRAYER INTO PRACTICE

The pilgrim, hermit or wanderer is one of our models for the search for wholeness—a model found in all religions. While the wanderer forgoes the comforts of home, he or she encounters the peace of profound silence and the joys of nature. Spend a little time, whenever you can, in silence or with nature.

PRAYER

Creator of the Cosmos,
Divine Designer,
your creation speaks of harmony and beauty.
The deeper I plunge myself into its mysteries
the more I perceive your presence.

CANTICLE Canticle of St. Patrick

Evening Prayer

Begin with page 79.

SCRIPTURE Matthew 8:20c

...but the Son of Man has nowhere to rest his head.

REFLECTION

Am I so caught up with my home that it is difficult for me to lose myself in the wonders of creation?

PRAYER

Almighty Artist,
you who paint the giraffes, the cardinals and the violets,
I sing your praises
and bask in the magnificence of your creation.

CANTICLE Canticle of St. Francis

Morning Prayer

Begin with page 78.

SCRIPTURE Matthew 5:14a, 16b

You are the light of the world.... [Y]our light must shine before others, that they may see your good deeds and glorify your heavenly Father.

WORDS OF WISDOM

A guru asked his disciples how they could tell when the night had ended and the day begun.

One said, "When you see an animal in the distance and can tell whether it is a cow or a horse."

"No," said the guru.

"When you look at a tree in the distance and can tell if it is a neem tree or a mango tree."

"Wrong again," said the guru.

"Well then, what is it?" asked the disciples.

"When you look into the face of any man and recognize your brother in him; when you look into the face of any woman and recognize in her your sister. If you cannot do this, no matter what time it is by the sun it is still night." (Anthony de Mello, S.J.)[1]

PRAYER

> Light of the world,
> help us to move
> from night to day.

CANTICLE Canticle of St. Francis

Evening Prayer

Begin with page 79.

SCRIPTURE *See page 88.*

REFLECTION

> In what way does my light shine before others?

PRAYER

> Only under the direction of your divine will
> do I develop the transparency needed to let your light
> shine.

> Glory be to the Father....

CANTICLE Canticle of Mary

Morning Prayer

Begin with page 78.

SCRIPTURE 1 Kings 10:1, 3, 6-9a

The Queen of Sheba, having heard of Solomon's fame, came to test him with subtle questions.... King Solomon explained everything she asked about, and there remained nothing hidden from him that he could not explain to her....

"The report I heard in my country about your deeds and your wisdom is true," she told the king. "Though I did not believe the report until I came and saw with my own eyes, I have discovered that they were not telling me the half. Your wisdom and prosperity surpass the report I heard. Happy are your men, happy these servants of yours, who stand before you always and listen to your word. Blessed be the LORD, your God, whom it has pleased to place you on the throne of Israel."

WORDS OF WISDOM

The time required to explore the wisdom of Solomon, as the Queen of Sheba did, no longer exists in what ecologist Jerry Rifkin calls our "nanosecond culture." Technique—*how* a thing is done (and how quickly) rather than *what* is done—has triumphed as "the sacred all-encompassing theme and guide," says Jacques Ellul, theologian and sociologist. Morals, ethics, spontaneity and personalism are swallowed up by our rapid-fire production mentality.

PRAYER

Creator of the Cosmos,
save me from the snares of the system we have created.
Free me from the maze of the machine,
which devalues human personality
in the pursuit of efficiency.
Help me bring heart into all my endeavors!

CANTICLE Canticle of St. Patrick

Evening Prayer

Begin with page 79.

SCRIPTURE *See page 90.*

REFLECTION

In what ways does our "nanosecond culture" interfere
with my relationships with coworkers, family and
friends?

PRAYER

You pour your wisdom upon me,
Divine Spirit.
Like a sponge, soft and porous,
I soak up your wise counsel.

CANTICLE Wisdom Canticle

Morning Prayer

Begin with page 78.

SCRIPTURE Mark 7:15, 21-23

Nothing that enters one from outside can defile that person; but the things that come out from within are what defile....

From within people, from their hearts, come evil thoughts, unchastity, theft, murder, adultery, greed, malice, deceit, licentiousness, envy's blasphemy, arrogance, folly. All these evils come from within and they defile.

WORDS OF WISDOM

St. John the Ladder, likening the methods of prayer to a ladder with four rungs, says, first we must wrestle with the mind and tame its passions; second, we must practice prayer with the lips, for, when passions are subdued, prayer quite naturally brings sweetness and enjoyment even to the tongue and is accepted by God as pleasing to Him; third, we must pray mentally; fourth, we must rise to contemplation. The first is appropriate to beginners, the second to those who have already achieved some measure of success; the third to those drawing close to the last rungs of achievement and the fourth to the perfect.

St. Simeon agrees that the only possible beginning is the diminishing and taming of passions. This is achieved in the soul by guarding the heart, for, as the Lord says, out of the heart proceed evil thoughts which defile a man. So it is there that attention and guarding are needful. When, through the heart's opposition to them, passions are completely subdued, the mind begins to long for God, seeking to get close to Him, for which purpose it increases its prayer.[2]

CANTICLE Canticle of Mary

Evening Prayer

Begin with page 79.

SCRIPTURE *See page 92.*

REFLECTION

How often today were you aware of your passion for something or someone?

PRAYER

Thank you, Christ,
for bringing us the consciousousness
to transform our lower nature to a higher one.

CANTICLE Wisdom Canticle

Opening Song for Morning Prayer

SALUTATION

> In eagerness I greet the sunrise,
> hopeful that I will hear your voice, Yahweh,
> in the events of the coming day.

SONG Psalm 95:1-6

> Come, let us sing joyfully to the LORD;
>   let us acclaim the Rock of our salvation.
> Let us greet him with thanksgiving;
>   let us joyfully sing psalms to him.
> For the LORD is a great God,
>   and a great king above all gods;
> In his hands are the depths of the earth,
>   and the tops of the mountains are his.
> His is the sea, for he has made it,
>   and the dry land which his hands have formed.
>
> Come, let us bow down in worship;
>   let us kneel before the LORD who made us.

Turn to the page with today's date for continuation of Morning Prayer.

Opening Song for Evening Prayer

SALUTATION

> Alone at night
> I seek the shelter of your strength,
> Creator God.

SONG Psalm 95:7-11

> For he is our God,
>> and we are the people he shepherds,
>>> the flock he guides.
> Oh, that today you would hear his voice:
>> "Harden not your hearts as at Meribah,
>> as in the day of Massah in the desert,
> Where your fathers tempted me;
>> they tested me though they had seen my works.
> Forty years I loathed that generation,
>> and I said: They are a people of erring heart,
>> and they know not my ways.
> Therefore I swore in my anger:
>> They shall not enter into my rest."

Turn to the page with today's date for the continuation of Evening Prayer.

Morning Prayer

Begin with page 94.

SCRIPTURE Mark 7:26-29

The woman was a Greek, a Syrophoenician by birth, and she begged Jesus to drive a demon out of her daughter. He said to her, "Let the children be fed first. For it is not right to take the food of the children and throw it to the dogs." She replied and said to him, "Lord, even the dogs under the table eat the children's scraps." Then he said to her, "For saying this, you may go. The demon has gone out of your daughter."

PRAYER

Grace me with the clarity
of the woman in today's Gospel,
who recognized the wisdom of your words
and the source of your spirit.

In perseverance and humility,
allow me to discern your truth today
before I make decisions and take action.

CANTICLE Canticle of Judith

Evening Prayer

Begin with page 95.

SCRIPTURE *See page 96.*

REFLECTION

Do I have the faith of the woman in today's Gospel—faith to reach for Christ's strength to overcome my human weaknesses?

PRAYER

You humbled yourself to teach me.
In humility, I sit at your feet to learn.

CANTICLE Wisdom Canticle

Morning Prayer

Begin with page 94.

SCRIPTURE Luke 11:2b-4

Father, hallowed be your name
your kingdom come.
Give us each day our daily bread
and forgive us our sins
for we ourselves forgive everyone in debt to us,
and do not subject us to the final test.

SPIRITUAL EXERCISE

Isn't it funny that the only thing expected from us in The
Lord's Prayer is to forgive one another? How much we
strive to build churches, set up charities, study
Scripture, and so on, when all along our main task is to
forgive one another.

If you can, spend a while meditating on this today. How
often do you get sidetracked into putting your energy
into projects and efforts to help others but fail to forgive
those within your own circle of family and friends?

PRAYER

How simple it is, Lord,
to know what you want.
But how difficult it is to do!

Help me to forgive
the slow, talkative clerk in the store,
the driver that cuts in front of me

and the child who won't do things my way.

Our Father....

CANTICLE Canticle of Mary

Evening Prayer

Begin with page 95.

SCRIPTURE Luke 11:4a, b

...and forgive us our sins
for we ourselves forgive everyone in debt to us....

REFLECTION

Have I forgiven everyone in debt to me? Do I stand in
need of forgiveness from another?

PRAYER

It is exciting, Spiritual Father,
to realize all the possibilities that exist each day
to serve you in many small ways.

Our Father....

CANTICLE Wisdom Canticle

Morning Prayer

Begin with page 94.

SCRIPTURE Luke 23:34b

Father, forgive them, they know not what they do.

WORDS OF WISDOM

A priest tells this story:

A few years ago, preparing to say a funeral Mass, I went into the side chapel for a short prayer. A woman sitting in the back of the chapel appeared quite agitated. In a few minutes she approached me and asked, "Father, did you know about the deceased's past?"

"Well no," I admitted.

"I was just wondering, with all she did and everything, if you think she made it," she asked, cocking her head in an upward fashion.

"God has great forgiveness," I answered with a smile. "You've heard the saying: The greater the sinner, the greater the saint?"

"Why no," replied the astonished woman. "I wish someone had told me that twenty years ago."

CANTICLE Canticle of Zechariah

Evening Prayer

Begin with page 95.

SCRIPTURE *See page 100.*

REFLECTION

Am I doing good things just to earn my way to heaven?

PRAYER

Help me to understand,
Forgiving God,
that living a life in the Spirit
is a reward in itself.

Our Father....

CANTICLE Canticle of Judith

Morning Prayer

Begin with page 94.

SCRIPTURE Matthew 5:22a

But I say to you, whoever is angry with his brother will be liable to judgment....

PUTTING PRAYER INTO PRACTICE

Anger kills. It is especially dangerous to the physical health of the angry person. Observe yourself today. When and to whom are you hostile? Get in touch with the roots of your anger.

PRAYER

Quiet my anxiety, Lord.
Bring peace to my hostile heart.
Teach me wisdom and understanding
so that I may be tranquil at all times.

CANTICLE Canticle of St. Patrick

Evening Prayer

Begin with page 95.

SCRIPTURE Matthew 5:22a

But I say to you, whoever is angry with his brother will be liable to judgment....

REFLECTION

In what situations do I react with uneasiness, fear or anger?

PRAYER

Divine Master, you have the power
to ease my troubled heart.
I only need to ask
and my spirit will be cleansed.

CANTICLE Wisdom Canticle

Morning Prayer

Begin with page 94.

SCRIPTURE John 5:30

I cannot do anything on my own; I judge as I hear, and my judgment is just, because I do not seek my own will but the will of the one who sent me.

WORDS OF WISDOM

He who has let himself be and who has let God be, lives in wandering joy, or joy without cause. (Meister Eckhart)[3]

PRAYER

Lord, lead my soul
to that spot of joy unceasing
where, because I walk in your will,
there is no cause for sorrow.

CANTICLE Canticle of St. Patrick

Evening Prayer

Begin with page 95.

SCRIPTURE *See page 104.*

REFLECTION

To what extent do I seek out my own will each day?

PRAYER

God of wisdom and mercy,
you are the architect of the universe.
I place my trust in you.

CANTICLE Wisdom Canticle

Morning Prayer

Begin with page 94.

SCRIPTURE James 1:16-18

Do not be deceived, my beloved brothers: all good giving
and every perfect gift is from above, coming down from
the Father of lights, with whom there is no alteration or
shadow caused by change. He willed to give us birth by
the word of truth that we may be a kind of first fruits of
his creatures.

PUTTING PRAYER INTO PRACTICE

Look at yourself in the mirror and love what you see. You
are, after all, God's creation and it may be a sin not to
accept yourself as you are. Admit your limitations and
celebrate your gifts.

PRAYER

Almighty Artist, Sculptor of the Spirit,
I am a masterwork of your creation,
a child of divine destiny.
You give me rare and wonderful gifts.
Today I celebrate the beauty of my being
and accept myself just as I am.

CANTICLE Canticle of Mary

Evening Prayer

Begin with page 95.

SCRIPTURE *See page 106.*

REFLECTION

How much confidence do I have in my own abilities?

PRAYER

Creator God,
you produce only originals.
Thank you for my uniqueness.
May I reflect your light and love.

CANTICLE Canticle of St. Francis

Morning Prayer

Begin with page 94.

SCRIPTURE James 1:2-4

Consider it all joy, my brothers, when you encounter various trials, for you know that the testing of your faith produces perseverance. And let perseverance be perfect, so that you may be perfect and complete, lacking in nothing.

PUTTING PRAYER INTO PRACTICE

The virtue of perseverance is always present where there is true love. Notice today in which areas and with which people you persevere.

PRAYER

God of love and compassion,
keep me from being tempted
by my own passions and desires.
Grant me the grace to give freely
and to love for the sheer delight of it!

CANTICLE Canticle of St. Patrick

Evening Prayer

Begin with page 95.

SCRIPTURE *See page 108.*

REFLECTION

In what ways was I tempted today? In what ways was my dedication or love put to the test? How did I react?

Enter your reflections in your spiritual journal, if you are keeping one.

PRAYER

Divine Lover,
hold me in your embrace
so that I may be one
with all creation.

CANTICLE Canticle of St. Francis

Opening Song for Morning Prayer

SALUTATION

My heart finds hope
in the promise
of a new day.

SONG Psalm 86:1-6

Incline your ear, O LORD; answer me,
    for I am afflicted and poor.
Keep my life, for I am devoted to you;
    save your servant who trusts in you.
You are my God; have pity on me, O Lord,
    for to you I call all the day.
Gladden the soul of your servant,
    for to you, O LORD, I lift up my soul;
For you, O Lord, are good and forgiving,
    abounding in kindness to all who call upon you.
Hearken, O LORD, to my prayer
    and attend to the sound of my pleading.

Turn to the page with today's date for the continuation of Morning Prayer.

Opening Song for Evening Prayer

SALUTATION

Lord of Light,
do not let the darkness
overcome me.

SONG Psalm 86:7-8, 15-16

In the day of my distress I call upon you,
for you will answer me.
There is none like you among the gods, O Lord,
and there are no works like yours....

But you, O Lord, are a God merciful and gracious,
slow to anger, abounding in kindness and fidelity.
Turn toward me, and have pity on me;
give your strength to your servant,
and save the son of your handmaid.

Turn to the page with today's date for the continuation of Evening Prayer.

Morning Prayer

Begin with page 110.

SCRIPTURE 1 Peter 4:1-2

Therefore, since Christ suffered in the flesh, arm yourselves also with the same attitude (for whoever suffers in the flesh has broken with sin), so as not to spend what remains of one's life in the flesh on human desires, but on the will of God.

COMMENTARY

Whole wheat bread was forced upon me at an early age. My mother simply quit buying the white. It was whole wheat or nothing. At first I didn't like it, but gradually I grew accustomed to the taste. Eventually, the healthy whole-grain bread became my natural choice.

Sin is like white bread (I'm talking about the small sins of selfishness that we get into as children and find hard to shake as we mature). At first it is all we know. But as we begin to reach out and take a few steps away from self, we find it's not so bad. The more we grow accustomed to loving our neighbors, even the ones we're not naturally fond of, the freer and healthier we feel. As we discipline ourselves for what is right and good, we begin to prefer it over sin.

CANTICLE Canticle of St. Patrick

Evening Prayer

Begin with page 111.

SCRIPTURE *See page 112.*

REFLECTION

In what ways have I broken with sin?

PRAYER

Brother Jesus,
you give the power to break with sin
and fall out of the line of least resistance.

Glory be to the Father....

CANTICLE Canticle of Mary

Morning Prayer

Begin with page 110.

SCRIPTURE Luke 6:41-42

Why do you notice the splinter in your brother's eye, but do not perceive the wooden beam in your own? How can you say to your brother, "Brother, let me remove that splinter in your eye," when you do not even notice the wooden beam in your own eye? You hypocrite! Remove the wooden beam from your eye first; then you will see clearly to remove the splinter in your brother's eye.

PUTTING PRAYER INTO PRACTICE

How often do we notice the splinter in another's eye—judging and condemning those souls whom we consider unworthy and banishing them from our neighborhoods, our churches and our lives.

Make an effort today to say a good word on the behalf of some group that is being labeled as no-good, lazy, crooked, pagan.

PRAYER

With your grace, Lord,
help me to seek my own healing,
to focus on my own brokenness,
and not that of my brothers and sisters.

CANTICLE Canticle of Judith

Evening Prayer

Begin with page 111.

SCRIPTURE *See page 114.*

REFLECTION

Did I speak up for the oppressed today and apply
criticism to my own faults?

PRAYER

You give us each other
to love and respect,
grand and glorious God.
I put my spirit-soul
into your hands
as I prepare to sleep. Amen.

CANTICLE Canticle of Mary

Morning Prayer

Begin with page 110.

SCRIPTURE John 16:32b-33

But I am not alone, because the Father is with me. I have told you this so that you might have peace in me. In the world you will have trouble, but take courage, I have conquered the world.

WORDS OF WISDOM

Julian of Norwich was a fourteenth-century anchoress, living in a cell attached to St. Julian's Church in Norwich, England. Her cell had two windows: one looking into the church and the other looking out on the world. Living in this tension between prayer and service she inspired many people during a time of disease, doom and social upheaval, with her best-known words: "All shall be well, and all manner of things shall be well." Hers was a voice of hope in an age of despair.

PRAYER

He said not,
"Thou shalt not be troubled;
thou shalt not be tempted;
thou shalt not be distressed."

He said,
"Thou shalt not be overcome."

CANTICLE Canticle of St. Francis

Evening Prayer

Begin with page 111.

SCRIPTURE *See page 116.*

REFLECTION

Am I a voice of hope in the midst of suffering?

PRAYER

For the strength, knowledge and faith
to overcome suffering
and be victorious over fear,
I pray in gratitude, Lord.

CANTICLE: Wisdom Canticle

Morning Prayer

Begin with page 110.

SCRIPTURE Matthew 5:44-45

But I say to you, love your enemies and pray for those who persecute you, that you may be children of your heavenly Father, for he makes his sun rise on the bad and the good, and causes rain to fall on the just and the unjust.

PUTTING PRAYER INTO PRACTICE

Let your love shine on all those who come within your presence, for love is not a commodity to be given or withheld, but an attitude: a reflection of the God-presence within you.

PRAYER

Just as the sun
can't help but shine,
so, too, may I love
because I can't do otherwise.

CANTICLE Canticle of St. Patrick

Evening Prayer

Begin with page 111.

SCRIPTURE Matthew 5:45b

...[F]or he makes his sun rise on the bad and the good, and causes rain to fall on the just and unjust.

REFLECTION

At what times do I withhold my love or compassion?

PRAYER

Spirit of wholeness,
you tenderly teach me
with your healing wand.
In you I rest and find peace.

Glory be to the Father....

CANTICLE Canticle of St. Francis

Morning Prayer

Begin with page 110.

SCRIPTURE Matthew 5:40

If anyone wants to go to law with you over your tunic, hand him your cloak as well.

PUTTING PRAYER INTO PRACTICE

Someone once said that practicing this passage in today's world would mean the following: If a thief broke into your home and stole your television set or other valuables, you would throw him the keys to your car so that he would have a vehicle with which to haul the loot away.

PRAYER

God of Light,
human attachment to things
brings darkness and grief.
May my acts
reflect care for your creatures
rather than passion for possessions.

CANTICLE Canticle of Zechariah

Evening Prayer

Begin with page 111.

SCRIPTURE *See page 120.*

REFLECTION

How do my possessions interfere with my relationships?

PRAYER

Your words, Lord, are harsh,
yet they give me the secret to happiness.
For your unfolding presence in my life,
I am indeed grateful.

CANTICLE Canticle of Judith

Morning Prayer

Begin with page 110.

SCRIPTURE Matthew 5:38-39

> You have heard that it was said, "An eye for an eye and a tooth for a tooth." But I say to you, offer no resistance to one who is evil. When someone strikes you on [your] right cheek, turn the other one to him as well.

COMMENTARY

> Resistance somehow interrupts the flow of divine providence. It is a mystery, but it seems that the Lord is telling us to trust that goodness will overcome evil.

PRAYER

> At first it seems strange, Christ,
> to turn the other cheek.
> But violence is contagious
> and only a strong warrior
> will have the power to deal
> with the conflict inside
> rather than pass it on.

CANTICLE Wisdom Canticle

Evening Prayer

Begin with page 111.

SCRIPTURE *See page 122.*

REFLECTION

What are the warring elements inside of me?

PRAYER

Christ, you teach me
to search my heart
for the source of conflict
rather than blame another.
For only when I win
the battle within myself
will I find peace.

CANTICLE Canticle of St. Francis

Morning Prayer

Begin with page 110.

SCRIPTURE Mark 9:35b

> If anyone wishes to be first, he shall be the last of all and the servant of all.

PUTTING PRAYER INTO PRACTICE

When you hear or read the word of God, pick out one sentence or phrase that strikes you and remember it during the day. Say the phrase silently to yourself and try to figure out how you can make the words come alive in your life. Today's Scripture is particularly suited to such an exercise; you will find ample opportunity to put it into practice.

PRAYER

Show me how, Lord,
to choose the place that is last.
Help me to
   give credit to others—eagerly,
   listen to another's opinion—attentively,
   wait in line—patiently,
   build your kingdom—cooperatively,
    with my fellow human beings.

CANTICLE Canticle of St. Patrick

Evening Prayer

Begin with page 111.

SCRIPTURE *See page 124.*

REFLECTION

In what ways was I willing to be last today?

PRAYER

You know, Lord,
that my selfishness demands
rewards and gratification.
Give me the grace, God, to be last.

CANTICLE Canticle of Mary

Opening Song for Morning Prayer

SALUTATION

> We adore you, O Christ;
> we bless you
> because by your holy cross
> you have redeemed the world.

SONG Psalm 32:1-5

> Happy is he whose fault is taken away,
>   whose sin is covered.
> Happy the man to whom the LORD imputes not guilt,
>   in whose spirit there is no guile.
>
> As long as I would not speak, my bones wasted away
>   with my groaning all the day,
> For day and night your hand was heavy upon me;
>   my strength was dried up as by the heat of summer.
> Then I acknowledged my sin to you,
>   my guilt I covered not.
> I said, "I confess my faults to the LORD,"
>   and you took away the guilt of my sin.

Turn to the page with today's date for the continuation of Morning Prayer.

Opening Song for Evening Prayer

SALUTATION

The night does not confound me,
for you, Lord, cover my shame
with the mantle of your mercy.

SONG Psalm 32:6-8, 11

For this shall every faithful man pray to you
    in time of stress.
Though deep waters overflow,
    they shall not reach him.
You are my shelter; from distress you will preserve me;
    with glad cries of freedom you will ring me round.

I will instruct you and show you the way you should
        walk;
    I will counsel you, keeping my eye on you....

Be glad in the LORD and rejoice, you just;
    exult, all you upright of heart.

Turn to the page with today's date for the continuation of Evening Prayer.

Morning Prayer

Begin with page 126.

SCRIPTURE Mark 9:47a

And if your eye causes you to sin, pluck it out.

PUTTING PRAYER INTO PRACTICE

We tend to think of these words as extreme, yet Christ
was pointing out that our souls (which are eternal) are of
much more importance than our eyes or hands (which
are only temporal). Yet how often do we sell our souls for
money, popularity or comfort? Watch for the times today
when you place material values above spiritual values.

PRAYER

Lead me, Lord,
to the knowledge
that life is much more
than a physical reality.

CANTICLE Wisdom Canticle

Evening Prayer

Begin with page 127.

SCRIPTURE Mark 9:47a

And if your eye causes you to sin, pluck it out.

REFLECTION

What opinions and emotions cut me off from grace?

PRAYER

You surround me with your caring,
Divine Trinity.
I yield to your wisdom
and rest in your strength,
Father, Son and Holy Spirit.

CANTICLE Canticle of Mary

Morning Prayer

Begin with page 126.

SCRIPTURE James 4:5-6

Or do you suppose that the scripture speaks without meaning when it says, "The spirit that he has made to dwell in us tends toward jealousy"? But he bestows a greater grace; therefore, it says:

"God resists the proud,
    but gives grace to the humble."

PUTTING PRAYER INTO PRACTICE

Catch yourself today when you tend toward jealousy.

PRAYER

I realize, Lord,
how the spirit of jealousy
can keep good people
at odds with one another.
Help me put my jealousy aside
so that I can join with others
to build your kingdom.

CANTICLE Canticle of Judith

Evening Prayer

Begin with page 127.

SCRIPTURE *See page 130.*

REFLECTION

Am I aware of how often jealousy interferes with my
goodness? At what times today did I become aware of my
jealousy? What were the causes?

*Enter your reflections in your spiritual journal, if you are
keeping one.*

PRAYER

According to Scripture,
even you are jealous sometimes, Lord.
Or is that just our human perception?
You give grace to the humble:
Lord, make me humble!

CANTICLE Canticle of Mary

Morning Prayer

Begin with page 126.

SCRIPTURE Matthew 6:1a, 3-4

...[T]ake care not to perform righteous deeds in order that people may see them.... But when you give alms, do not let your left hand know what your right is doing, so that your almsgiving may be secret. And your Father who sees in secret will repay you.

WORDS OF WISDOM

It is easy in the world to live after the world's opinion; it is easy in solitude to live after our own; but the great man is he who in the midst of the crowd keeps with perfect sweetness the independence of solitude. (Ralph Waldo Emerson)

PRAYER

May my giving be like the sun's shining:
    something I do naturally
    with no thought of return.

CANTICLE Canticle of St. Patrick

Evening Prayer

Begin with page 127.

SCRIPTURE *See page 132.*

REFLECTION

Do I help others at *my* convenience?

PRAYER

In my weakness,
you show me mercy and compassion.
You ease my burdens when I cry for help.
I am in awe of such love and fidelity.

Glory be to the Father....

CANTICLE Canticle of Mary

Morning Prayer

Begin with page 126.

SCRIPTURE Matthew 6:25, 33-34a

Therefore I tell you, do not worry about your life, what
you will eat [or drink], or about your body, what you will
wear. Is not life more than food and the body more than
clothing?... But seek first the kingdom [of God] and his
righteousness, and all these things will be given you
besides. Do not worry about tomorrow; tomorrow will
take care of itself.

PUTTING PRAYER INTO PRACTICE

If a homeless person said the above words to a
middle-class homeowner, what would be the
homeowner's reaction? Christ was homeless two
thousand years ago when he spoke these words.

Meditate now on what aspects of your life are motivated
by the desire for food, shelter, clothing and security.
When you are compassionate and caring, what attitude
motivates you? When you are defensive and closed, what
attitude motivates you? Practice this routine every day if
you can. Lent is an especially good time to start.

CANTICLE Canticle of St. Patrick

Evening Prayer

Begin with page 127.

SCRIPTURE Matthew 6:34a

Do not worry about tomorrow; tomorrow will take care of itself.

REFLECTION

At what times today did I feel compassion?

PRAYER

Brother Jesus,
you show me that
when I make love and truth
my top priority,
God will provide for me.
I understand, too,
that misfortune, disease and death
are also part of a fulfilling life.
Help me to find your peace
in both the bitter and the sweet.

CANTICLE Wisdom Canticle

Morning Prayer

Begin with page 126.

SCRIPTURE 1 Peter 1:24-25

All flesh is like grass
   and all its glory like the flower of the field;
the grass withers,
   and the flower wilts;
but the word of the Lord remains forever.

CENTERING PRAYER

Sit in a relaxed position with your back straight. Close
your eyes and say The Lord's Prayer slowly. Slow your
breathing as much as possible. When you finish The
Lord's Prayer take up your prayer word and say it over
and over in rhythm with your breathing. Whenever it
feels right, let go of the word and rest in the presence of
the Lord, who is the center of your being. When you are
distracted, take up your prayer word again to help you
return to the center.

To come out of prayer, end with The Lord's Prayer.

Since it takes most people several minutes to unwind and
get into a proper prayer posture, this prayer requires a
minimum of five to ten minutes. As you get comfortable
with the silence and stillness, extend the time to suit
your own prayer pace.

CANTICLE Canticle of St. Patrick

Evening Prayer

Begin with page 127.

SCRIPTURE 1 Peter 1:25b

...[T]he word of the Lord remains forever.

REFLECTION

My prayer word has power. How do I choose to channel this power in my life?

PRAYER

You who are my center,
my reason for being,
grace me with the discipline
and the desire
to use my centering prayer daily.

CANTICLE Canticle of Mary

Morning Prayer

Begin with page 126.

SCRIPTURE Matthew 23:25-26

Woe to you, scribes and Pharisees, you hypocrites. You cleanse the outside of cup and dish, but inside they are full of plunder and self-indulgence. Blind Pharisee, cleanse first the inside of the cup, so that the outside also may be clean.

PUTTING PRAYER INTO PRACTICE

Where did we get the idea that cleanliness is next to godliness? Actually, our fastidiousness can keep us from one another. How often does the fear of bugs, germs, dirt, disorder, disease or offensive odors keep you from getting involved with the poor or the sick? Watch for that today.

PRAYER

Lead me, Lord,
into the interior of my being.
Deliver me from my superficial concerns
for cleanliness and control.

CANTICLE Canticle of Mary

Evening Prayer

Begin with page 127.

SCRIPTURE *See page 138.*

REFLECTION

Did I withdraw from anyone today because of my need
for cleanliness?

PRAYER

Brother Jesus,
you remind me of what is important,
whereas the world chases after appearances.
You inspire and console my inner spirit.

Glory be to the Father....

CANTICLE Canticle of St. Francis

Morning Prayer

Begin with page 126.

SCRIPTURE Proverbs 17:1

Better a dry crust with peace
than a house full of feasting with strife.

PUTTING PRAYER INTO PRACTICE

No food tastes as wonderful as the bread and cheese
eaten on the side of a mountain after a long hike up.
Notice today how peace accompanies natural, simple
living, while strife accompanies extravagance.

PRAYER

Excess and extravagance
rob me of reality.
Empty me then, Divine Master,
of everything except you.

CANTICLE Canticle of Mary

Evening Prayer

Begin with page 127.

SCRIPTURE Proverbs 17:1

> Better a dry crust with peace
> than a house full of feasting with strife.

REFLECTION

Am I aware of at least one area in my life that is cluttered and complicated? Does it cause strife?

PRAYER

Brother Jesus,
you enjoyed life
without living extravagantly.
Thank you for your example
of the sweetness of simplicity.

CANTICLE Canticle of Judith

Morning Prayer

Begin with page 126.

COMMENTARY

To make a complete solar journey, it takes the planet earth three hundred sixty five days, five hours, forty-eight minutes and forty-five seconds. Consequently, after each year of three hundred sixty-five days, there is some time left over. Every four years, this accumulated time is used up by adding one more day to the year. February 29, then, "leaps" over excess time.

SCRIPTURE Malachi 3:19-21

For lo, the day is coming, blazing like an oven,
    when all the proud and all evildoers will be stubble,
And the day that is coming will set them on fire,
    leaving them neither root nor branch,
    says the LORD of hosts.

But for you who fear my name, there will arise
    the sun of justice with its healing rays;
And you will gambol like calves out of the stall
    and tread down the wicked;
They will become ashes under the soles of your feet,
    on the day I take action, says the LORD of hosts.

PUTTING PRAYER INTO PRACTICE

Leap over obstacles and negative feelings by making love the ruling force of your day. If someone offends you, recognize that the offense came out of that person's need or sense of lack. Rather than return injury for injury, act with a positive, loving response that fills the other's need. This kind of love generates amazing power.

PRAYER

By my words and actions today,
May I sow seeds of divine love.

CANTICLE Canticle of Mary

Evening Prayer

Begin with page 127.

SCRIPTURE Malachi 3:20b

And you will gambol like calves out of the stall.

REFLECTION

When were my responses positive and loving? What were the effects?

PRAYER

Gentle Mystery,
your love fills me
and surrounds me.
I rest in you.

CANTICLE Wisdom Canticle

Notes

[1] Excerpt from *The Prayer of the Frog: A Book of Story Meditations*, copyright ©1988 by Anthony de Mello, S.J., is reprinted with permission of Gujarat Sahitya Prakash, Anand, India.

[2] Excerpt from *Writings From the Philokalia on Prayer of the Heart*, copyright ©1951 by Faber & Faber, is used with permission of the publisher.

[3] Excerpt from *Breakthrough: Meister Eckhart's Creation Spirituality*, copyright ©1980 by Matthew Fox, is used by permission of Image Books, Doubleday & Company.

March

Opening Song for Morning Prayer

SALUTATION

At daybreak my heart rejoices at the word of the Lord.

SONG Song of Songs 4:16

Arise, north wind! Come, south wind!
  blow upon my garden,
    that its perfumes may spread abroad.
Let my lover come to his garden,
  and eat its choice fruits.

Turn to the page with today's date for the continuation of Morning Prayer.

Opening Song for Evening Prayer

SALUTATION

> The night wraps around me
> like a warm, comfortable cloak,
> restoring my soul
> with calm and rest.

SONG Psalm 16:7-11

> I bless the LORD who counsels me;
>> even in the night my heart exhorts me.
> I set the LORD ever before me;
>> with him at my right hand I shall not be disturbed.
> Therefore my heart is glad and my soul rejoices,
>> my body, too, abides in confidence;
> Because you will not abandon my soul to the nether
>> world,
>> nor will you suffer your faithful one to undergo
>> corruption.
> You will show me the path to life,
>> fullness of joys in your presence,
>> the delights at your right hand forever.

Turn to the page with today's date for the continuation of Evening Prayer.

Morning Prayer

Begin with page 146.

SCRIPTURE Luke 8:25c

...Who then is this, who commands even the winds and the sea, and they obey him?

MEDITATION

What does the wind symbolize for you? Does it remind you of the Holy Spirit or of God's fury?

Sometime today, sit in silence near a partially opened window. Listen to the wind or the breeze. Listen with full concentration. Let the sound envelope you. What is its message?

PRAYER

The wind whispers its secret
to those who are ready to hear it.
Happiness rides on the gusts
that blow free
because they have developed the grace
to let go.

CANTICLE Canticle of Judith

Evening Prayer

Begin with page 147.

SCRIPTURE *See page 148.*

REFLECTION

How am I dealing with the turbulence inside me? How can I allow God to bring calm to my inner life?

PRAYER

Christ, you command the wind
and calm the chaos in my nature.

Glory be to the Father....

CANTICLE Canticle of St. Patrick

Morning Prayer

Begin with page 146.

SCRIPTURE Luke 9:24

> For whoever wishes to save his life will lose it, but whoever loses his life for my sake will save it.

PUTTING PRAYER INTO PRACTICE

> Christ turns our world upside down. Human logic and values are often the opposite of supernatural values. As you journey through your day, remember that what you grasp will elude you and what you give freely for Christ's sake will be returned.

PRAYER

> Restore my soul
> to a place of harmony,
> where I am in balance
> to give and receive.

CANTICLE Canticle of Mary

Evening Prayer

Begin with page 147.

SCRIPTURE *See page 150.*

REFLECTION

What are some ways in which I can lose my life?

Enter your reflections in your spiritual journal, if you are keeping one.

PRAYER

Lord, you give me the free will
to accept or reject your gifts.
I rejoice in my freedom to come to you
out of love rather than fear.

Glory be to the Father....

CANTICLE Canticle of St. Francis

Morning Prayer

Begin with page 146.

SCRIPTURE 1 Corinthians 9:24-27

Do you not know that the runners in the stadium all run in the race, but only one wins the prize? Run so as to win. Every athlete exercises discipline in every way. They do it to win a perishable crown, but we an imperishable one. Thus I do not run aimlessly; I do not fight as if I were shadowboxing. No, I drive my body and train it, for fear that, after having preached to others, I myself should be disqualified.

PUTTING PRAYER INTO PRACTICE

Better to be a sincere street sweeper than a phony pastor! Whatever you do today, give it all you've got. No matter how humble the task, throw yourself into it.

PRAYER

Lord of Light,
lead me to my highest self,
so that I may be inspired
always to do my best.

CANTICLE Canticle of St. Patrick

Evening Prayer

Begin with page 147.

SCRIPTURE 1 Corinthians 9:24b

Run so as to win.

REFLECTION

How often do I run the race for a crown that will perish?

PRAYER

Thank you, God,
for reminding me always
to put my energies into loving
both brother and sister,
for love is the crown
that will not perish.

CANTICLE Canticle of Mary

Morning Prayer

Begin with page 146.

SCRIPTURE Esther C:14b

My LORD, our King, you alone are God. Help me, who am alone and have no help but you, for I am taking my life in my hand.

MEDITATION

What can we hang onto? We cannot hang onto personal relationships, for they perish. We cannot hang onto romantic love, it satisfies only temporarily. Alone, the Infinite remains.

What is the Infinite to you? Get in touch with your idea of the infinite Spirit and hang onto that.

PRAYER

God, I grasp your greatness.
I rest in the peace
that there is something greater than myself.
I sit now in silence
to draw strength
from your infinite source.

Silence

CANTICLE Canticle of Judith

Evening Prayer

Begin with page 147.

SCRIPTURE *See page 154.*

REFLECTION

How many times do I fail to draw strength from the Infinite but think, instead, that I have to rely on my own resources? Conversely, how many times do I depend too much on the Infinite rather than being resourceful myself?

PRAYER

In your deep stillness,
I rest my soul
and relax my body.

CANTICLE Wisdom Canticle

Morning Prayer

Begin with page 146.

SCRIPTURE Hosea 13:15

> Though he be fruitful among his fellows,
>> an east wind shall come, a wind from the LORD,
>> rising from the desert,
> That shall dry up his spring,
>> and leave his fountain dry.
> It shall loot his land
>> of every precious thing.

PUTTING PRAYER INTO PRACTICE

Lent is a time of dryness. Even when we seek God, God sometimes chooses to leave us in desolation rather than console us. If we lose heart easily, we are still like children, looking for rewards.

There will be situations in which you will have the opportunity to choose the better way even though it may involve personal loss. Such situations may require refusing to gossip, refusing to put someone down, speaking out against prejudice and so on.

PRAYER

May I respond to others
with a humble heart
and a meek spirit.

CANTICLE Canticle of St. Patrick

Evening Prayer

Begin with page 147.

SCRIPTURE *See page 156.*

REFLECTION

Did I overcome a difficult or trying situation today with
humility?

PRAYER

For the faith
to move through the darkness
unafraid,
I thank you, Lord.

CANTICLE Canticle of Zechariah

Morning Prayer

Begin with page 146.

SCRIPTURE 2 Timothy 1:8b-9a

[B]ear your share of hardship for the gospel with the strength that comes from God.

He saved us and called us to a holy life....

WORDS OF WISDOM

The fundamental law of morality for [Pierre] Teilhard [de Chardin] was to liberate that conscious energy, which seeks to further unify the world. He calls this energy the zest for life—that disposition of mind and heart that savors the experience of life, and manifests itself particularly in the relish a man has for creative tasks undertaken from a sense of duty. His life, in a true sense, has ceased to be private to him. Body and soul, he is the product of a huge creative work with which the totality of things has collaborated from the beginning. If he refuses the task assigned to him, some part of that effort will be lost forever....[1]

PRAYER

Teach me to listen, all-knowing God
so that I may hear my holy calling
and carry out my appointed task.

CANTICLE Canticle of Zechariah

Evening Prayer

Begin with page 147.

SCRIPTURE *See page 158.*

REFLECTION

Do I have the qualities of a good listener?

If you are keeping a spiritual journal, list the qualities of a good listener and check off the ones you have. Enter your own suggestions on how you can develop listening qualities that you do not have.

PRAYER

In the quiet of the night
I listen for your voice,
O Music of the Universe.

CANTICLE Wisdom Canticle

Morning Prayer

Begin with page 146.

SCRIPTURE 1 Samuel 3:10c

Speak, for your servant is listening.

PUTTING PRAYER INTO PRACTICE

Developing good listening skills is an important part of
prayer. It cultivates an attitude of openness and patience.
Practice good listening habits with the people you meet
today. When you listen, set aside your own needs and
anxieties, your judgments and your thoughts about what
you are going to say next. Pay attention to the words and
feelings of the speaker. As you grow in your ability to
listen to others, you grow in your ability to listen to God.

PRAYER

Am I really listening to you, Lord,
or just mouthing the words?
Do I sincerely want to hear
what you have to say to me,
or do I just want to tell
you what I need?
Be patient with me, Lord,
as your servant strives
to learn to listen.

CANTICLE Canticle of St. Patrick

Evening Prayer

Begin with page 147.

SCRIPTURE 1 Samuel 3:10

Speak, for your servant is listening.

REFLECTION

Did I become aware today of some attitude or behavior in myself that keeps me from being a good listener?

PRAYER

Compassionate Creator,
I am grateful
for your understanding
and patience.

Glory be to the Father....

CANTICLE Wisdom Canticle

Opening Song for Morning Prayer

SALUTATION Isaiah 58:10

> If you bestow your bread on the hungry
> > and satisfy the afflicted;
> Then light shall rise for you in the darkness,
> > and the gloom shall become for you like midday....

SONG Isaiah 58:3b-5

> Lo, on your fast day you carry out your own pursuits,
> > and drive all your laborers.
> Yes, your fast ends in quarreling and fighting,
> > striking with wicked claw.
> Would that today you might fast
> > so as to make your voice heard on high!
> Is this the manner of fasting I wish,
> > of keeping a day of penance:
> That a man bow his head like a reed,
> > and lie in sackcloth and ashes?
> Do you call this a fast,
> > a day acceptable to the LORD?

Turn to the page with today's date for the continuation of Morning Prayer.

Opening Song for Evening Prayer

SALUTATION

As dusk descends
my heart longs for the Lord
and my spirit rejoices in prayer!

SONG Isaiah 58:6-7

This, rather, is the fasting that I wish:
  releasing those bound unjustly,
  untying the thongs of the yoke;
Setting free the oppressed,
  breaking every yoke;
Sharing your bread with the hungry,
  sheltering the oppressed and the homeless;
Clothing the naked when you see them,
  and not turning your back on your own.

Turn to the page with today's date for the continuation of Evening Prayer.

Morning Prayer

Begin with page 162.

SCRIPTURE Hosea 14:4b

> We shall say no more, "Our God,"
>   to the work of our hands;
>   for in you the orphan finds compassion.

WORDS OF WISDOM

> Security is mostly a superstition. It does not exist in
> nature, nor do the children of [the earth] as a whole
> experience it. Avoiding danger is no safer than outright
> exposure. Life is either a daring adventure or it is
> nothing. (Helen Keller)[2]

PRAYER

> Lower my guard, God.
> Let me dare to love
> and run the risk
> of inspired adventure.

CANTICLE Canticle of Judith

Evening Prayer

Begin with page 163.

SCRIPTURE *See page 164.*

REFLECTION

At which things do I grasp for security?

PRAYER

Brother Jesus,
you bring us a deeper reality
and show us the futility of grasping.
I end my prayer
in gratefulness for your generosity,
Giver of life.

CANTICLE Canticle of St. Francis

Morning Prayer

Begin with page 162.

SCRIPTURE Matthew 4:1-2

Then Jesus was led by the Spirit into the desert to be tempted by the devil. He fasted for forty days and forty nights, and afterwards he was hungry.

PUTTING PRAYER INTO PRACTICE

Fasting can spiritually transform you if you accompany your fast with prayer and an attitude of openness. Going without food frees the body from the burden of digestion and allows energy to take a spiritual direction, if the mind so wills it. Eating is a baby's first act of selfishness. Denying yourself food as an adult empties you not only of food but of "self" and gives the spirit room. On a day when you can pray, go without food for several hours, even the whole day. Take fruit juice if you feel weak. Your body may crave food, but your soul will be nourished!

PRAYER

When I am hungry,
when I am weak,
then I am one
with the least
of my brothers and sisters.

CANTICLE Canticle of Mary

Evening Prayer

Begin with page 163.

SCRIPTURE *See page 166.*

REFLECTION

From what I know of Christ in the Scriptures, why does he ask me to fast? Why does he ask me to pray? How often does he ask me to help the poor and weak?

PRAYER

Son of Man,
you show me how
to rise above
my physical nature.

CANTICLE Canticle of Zechariah

Morning Prayer

Begin with page 162.

SCRIPTURE Jonah 3:1-5, 10

The word of the LORD came to Jonah a second time: "Set out for the great city of Nineveh, and announce to it the message that I will tell you." So Jonah made ready and went to Nineveh, according to the LORD's bidding. Now Nineveh was an enormously large city; it took three days to go through it. Jonah began his journey through the city, and had gone but a single day's walk announcing, "Forty days more and Nineveh shall be destroyed," when the people of Nineveh believed God; they proclaimed a fast and all of them, great and small, put on sackcloth.

...When God saw by their actions how they turned from their evil way, he repented of the evil that he had threatened to do to them; he did not carry it out.

PUTTING PRAYER INTO PRACTICE

Nineveh was headed for destruction until its people accepted Jonah as a sign from God and changed their course. Today, destruction often occurs within the family unit when members fail to treat each other gently and lovingly. To bind your family together, suggest that everyone spend five minutes together, twice a week, in silence. It is important that each member views this time as a commitment and allows nothing else to take priority. During this time, hold hands in silence. You can light a candle or dim the lights if you prefer, but just experience being together as a family in peace and quiet. Once this seed of silent togetherness is planted, you will be amazed at the fruit it bears—provided you stick to the schedule.

PRAYER

The sound of silence
heals and harmonizes
through its message of peace.

CANTICLE Canticle of Judith

Evening Prayer

Begin with page 163.

SCRIPTURE *See page 168.*

REFLECTION

How do I treat people? Am I sensitive to their needs?

PRAYER

You give me the gift of silence
with its message of peace and patience.
And to receive it, I only have to turn off
everything else.

CANTICLE Wisdom Canticle

Morning Prayer

Begin with page 162.

SCRIPTURE Psalm 46:11a

Desist! and confess that I am God....

PUTTING PRAYER INTO PRACTICE

A parish priest once speculated that if Christ walked into church, we would all "get busy" because when we're busy we think we are good. Because busyness is so often equated with goodness, we sometimes consider prayer a waste of time. Actually, prayer is the highest form of "doing."

Developing concentration to the point where one can turn off bodily needs, passions, worries, ego, and concentrate on listening and being in harmony with the life-giving consciousness of the universe is the most difficult of all accomplishments.

PRAYER

Healer of my Soul,
still my imagination.
Relieve me of anxiety
so that I may be in
communion with you.

Silence

CANTICLE Canticle of St. Patrick

Evening Prayer

Begin with page 163.

SCRIPTURE Psalm 46:11a

Desist! and confess that I am God....

REFLECTION

What are the things that distract me from sitting in stillness and waiting upon the Lord?

PRAYER

Always, I can close my eyes
and find you, Divine Healer,
in the stillness of my soul.

Glory be to the Father....

CANTICLE Canticle of St. Francis

Morning Prayer

Begin with page 162.

SCRIPTURE Matthew 4:4b

> One does not live by bread alone,
> but by every word that comes forth
> from the mouth of God.

PUTTING PRAYER INTO PRACTICE

Christ is like a pineapple upside-down cake, according to one pastor. What appears to be plain and ordinary from outward appearance turns out to be wonderful—full of fruit and pleasing to the palate. Christ's message shows us the flip side of God; Christ overturns the world's values with divine truth. He shows us things we would never see with human perspective.

PRAYER

> Today, Brother Jesus,
> help me to view the world
> from your perspective,
> seeing what is invisible
> and hearing what goes unsaid.

CANTICLE Canticle of St. Patrick

Evening Prayer

Begin with page 163.

SCRIPTURE Matthew 4:4b

One does not live by bread alone,
but by every word that comes forth
from the mouth of God.

REFLECTION

What does the word *bread* as used in today's Scripture
selection mean to me? What are some other words I
could substitute for the word *bread*?

PRAYER

Your word, Lord,
brings nourishment to my soul.
I delight in your decrees.

CANTICLE Wisdom Canticle

Morning Prayer

Begin with page 162.

SCRIPTURE Isaiah 1:16c-17a

[C]ease doing evil; learn to do good.

PUTTING PRAYER INTO PRACTICE

Focus on doing good and you will gradually become aware of the evil you engage in. This evil will automatically and gradually cease as your awareness grows. Today, do not focus on your faults. Instead, focus on every opportunity to be loving, generous, honest, open and gentle.

PRAYER

I am surrounded,
Gentle God,
with opportunities
to be a vessel of your compassion.
Help me to see and seize
each chance to be kind.

CANTICLE Canticle of St. Patrick

Evening Prayer

Begin with page 163.

SCRIPTURE Isaiah 1:16c-17a

[C]ease doing evil; learn to do good.

REFLECTION

In what ways did I learn to do good today?

PRAYER

In gratefulness for the wisdom
and the grace to learn to do good,
I thank you,
Giver of all good things.

CANTICLE Canticle of Judith

Morning Prayer

Begin with page 162.

SCRIPTURE Hosea 8:7

When they sow the wind,
   they shall reap the whirlwind;
The stalk of grain that forms no ear
   can yield no flour;
Even if it could,
   strangers would swallow it.

PUTTING PRAYER INTO PRACTICE

Our efforts are in vain if we have lost our sense of vision
or purpose. Be aware of your efforts today and ask
yourself, "Why am I doing this?"

PRAYER

Make me mindful, Master,
of my purpose on this planet.
May my decisions and actions
enhance dignity and respect
for you and your creatures.

CANTICLE Canticle of St. Patrick

Evening Prayer

Begin with page 163.

SCRIPTURE *See page 176.*

REFLECTION

How happy am I with the answers I gave myself when I asked the question, "Why am I doing this?"

PRAYER

It's sometimes easy for me
to discount my efforts
by thinking I'm not important enough
to be responsible
or to make a difference.
Vanquish my apathy
and fill me with your vision, God,
so that I may claim my rightful inheritance
as a child of God.

CANTICLE Canticle of Mary

Opening Song for Morning Prayer

SALUTATION

Come, morning light,
as creation gives birth
to a new day.

SONG Psalm 5:1-3, 11-12

Hearken to my words, O LORD,
    attend to my sighing.
Heed my call for help,
    my king and my God!
To you I pray, O LORD,
    at dawn you hear my voice;
    at dawn I bring my plea expectantly before you.

...Punish them, O God;
    let them fall by their own devices;
For their many sins cast them out
    because they have rebelled against you.
But let all who take refuge in you
    be glad and exult forever.
Protect them, that you may be the joy
    of those who love your name.

*Turn to the page with today's date for the continuation of
Morning Prayer.*

Opening Song for Evening Prayer

SALUTATION

In the name of Jesus Christ,
I empty my mind of its cares and burdens
and take refuge in God's love.

SONG Psalm 13:2-6

How long O LORD? Will you utterly forget me?
How long will you hide your face from me?
How long shall I harbor sorrow in my soul,
grief in my heart day after day?
How long will my enemy triumph over me?
Look, answer me, O LORD, my God!

Give light to my eyes that I may not sleep in death
lest my enemy say, "I have overcome him";
Lest my foes rejoice at my downfall
though I trusted in your kindness.
Let my heart rejoice in your salvation;
Let me sing of the LORD, "He has been good to me."

Turn to the page with today's date for the continuation of Evening Prayer.

Morning Prayer

Begin with page 178.

SCRIPTURE John 4:13b-14a

Everyone who drinks this water will be thirsty again; but whoever drinks the water I shall give will never thirst....

PUTTING PRAYER INTO PRACTICE

We all thirst for more than water. Love, attention, knowledge, power, riches, pleasure—these are some of the things we thirst after. Abstain from water today for as long as you are able. Let your thirst remind you of your deepest thirst—connection with the source of living water.

PRAYER

O you who are the Divine Drink,
flood my dry spirit
with your living water.
Quench my thirst for belonging.

CANTICLE Canticle of Judith

Evening Prayer

Begin with page 179.

SCRIPTURE John 4:14a

But whoever drinks the water I shall give will never thirst....

REFLECTION

In what ways did God fill my cup today?

PRAYER

You are the fountain of hope,
the water of life,
generous God.

Glory be to the Father....

CANTICLE Canticle of St. Francis

Morning Prayer

Begin with page 178.

SCRIPTURE Daniel 13:23

(If you have time, read all of Daniel 13. It is a fascinating story!)

Yet it is better for me to fall into your power without guilt than to sin before the Lord.

PUTTING PRAYER INTO PRACTICE

Many of our problems stem from our need for immediate gratification. Because we want to satisfy our desire for excitement, comfort, pleasure and so on, we refuse to acknowledge the consequences of our actions. Look out today for the times you are satisfying an immediate need in a way that could lead to future problems.

PRAYER

Keep me from discouragement, Lord,
as I become more and more aware
of my compulsions and instant wants.
Help me rejoice in the knowledge
that only the mature can laugh
and let go of childish demands.

CANTICLE Canticle of St. Francis

Evening Prayer

Begin with page 179.

SCRIPTURE *See page 182.*

REFLECTION

In what ways do I make hasty decisions to satisfy myself?

If you are keeping a spiritual journal, keep track, as you grow in awareness, of your impulsive ways.

PRAYER

Like a laughing child,
I run into your arms
and rest my head on your shoulder.

CANTICLE Wisdom Canticle

Morning Prayer

Begin with page 178.

SCRIPTURE Matthew 24:42-44

Therefore, stay awake! For you do not know on which day your Lord will come. Be sure of this: if the master of the house had known the hour of night when the thief was coming, he would have stayed awake and not let his house be broken into. So too, you also must be prepared, for at an hour you do not expect, the Son of Man will come.

PUTTING PRAYER INTO PRACTICE

Be alert today. Do not say anything in secret about someone that you would not say to his or her face. Think about this before you speak!

PRAYER

Help me, Lord, to be honest
and act with integrity at all times.
Give me the grace to be prepared
to meet you at any hour.

Glory be to the Father....

CANTICLE Canticle of St. Patrick

Evening Prayer

Begin with page 179.

SCRIPTURE *See page 184.*

REFLECTION

Was I caught off guard today? Did I say something that I would be ashamed of before the Son of Man?

PRAYER

Thank you for this time of reflection during Lent—
a time to pray and prepare a place in my heart
for Christ-consciousness,
for unconditional love,
for the Son of Man.
Thank you, God, Father and Mother.

CANTICLE Canticle of Zechariah

Morning Prayer

Begin with page 178.

SCRIPTURE Matthew 26:21b, 24

Amen, I say to you, one of you will betray me.... The Son of Man indeed goes, as it is written of him, but woe to that man by whom the Son of Man is betrayed. It would be better for that man if he had never been born.

PUTTING PRAYER INTO PRACTICE

Lent is the time to look at our sins. There are many definitions of sin. Two of my favorites come from my pastor: (1) Sin is my failure to love or forgive. (2) Sin is my use or misuse of someone or something for my own selfish purposes. What is your definition of sin? Apply it to your actions today.

PRAYER

Each day, Brother Jesus,
I betray you in some way.
Forgive me for my ignorance and weakness.

Our Father....

CANTICLE Canticle of Judith

Evening Prayer

Begin with page 178.

SCRIPTURE *See page 186.*

REFLECTION

According to your own definition of sin, how did you sin today? Write your definition of sin in your spiritual journal, if you are keeping one.

PRAYER

Your forgiveness is infinite;
your mercy abounds.
You are all that can be
and I rejoice in your being.

CANTICLE Wisdom Canticle

Morning Prayer

Begin with page 178.

SCRIPTURE Matthew 1:18b-21

When...Mary was betrothed to Joseph, but before they
lived together, she was found with child through the
holy Spirit. Joseph, her husband, since he was a
righteous man, yet unwilling to expose her to shame,
decided to divorce her quietly. Such was his intention
when, behold, the angel of the Lord appeared to him in a
dream and said, "Joseph, son of David, do not be afraid to
take Mary your wife into your home. For it is through the
holy Spirit that this child has been conceived in her. She
will bear a son and you are to name him Jesus, because
he will save his people from their sins."

CANTICLE AND PRAYER Joseph's Song

Yahweh, am I to understand
that the Anointed One,
the One Israel awaits,
will come during my life?
And that into my humble hands
you want to entrust
the incarnation of your love?

Such divine destiny is more than I can bear.
The risk is as great as the honor,
but how could it be otherwise?
No, it must be a trick!
Only pride would presume such a charge.
Yet, I cannot deny the dream or in Mary find fault.

In the Lord I place my confidence and trust.
For it is only in his strength that I can overcome
the fear of this awesome responsibility.

Generation after generation will struggle
for the meaning of the Lamb of God
but only those who dare to *risk*
will hold the promise in their arms.

Evening Prayer

Begin with page 178.

SCRIPTURE *See page 188.*

REFLECTION

Do I ever refuse to listen to God's voice because I fear
the responsibility to which God may be calling me?

CANTICLE AND PRAYER Joseph's Song (page 188)

Morning Prayer

Begin with page 178.

SCRIPTURE John 8:7b

Let the one among you who is without sin be the first to throw a stone at her.

PUTTING PRAYER INTO PRACTICE

Your sins will find you out. If you are reading this book, chances are you have a well-developed conscience. You must answer not only to God and your own fellow humans, but also to your own sense of personal integrity. Those things that are obstacles to your "fullness in the Spirit" find you each day. You will know them when you feel impatient or threatened. Today when they find you, listen and learn from them.

PRAYER

Help me listen, Lord,
to the voice within.
Restrain me from filling my world
with the din and screech of human noise
in order to drown out the sound
of my conscience.

CANTICLE Wisdom Canticle

Evening Prayer

Begin with page 179.

SCRIPTURE John 8:7b

Let the one among you who is without sin be the first to throw a stone at her.

REFLECTION

Did I learn anything about the obstacles that are keeping me from a closer relationship with God?

PRAYER

Whatever temptation or disaster befalls,
I am secure and grateful
for that inner sanctuary within my being
where I can dwell
in the presence of God.

CANTICLE Canticle of Mary

Morning Prayer

Begin with page 178.

SCRIPTURE John 13:12-15

So when he had washed their feet [and] put his garments back on and reclined at table again, he said to them, "Do you realize what I have done for you? You call me 'teacher' and 'master,' and rightly so, for indeed I am. If I, therefore, the master and teacher, have washed your feet, you ought to wash one another's feet. I have given you a model to follow, so that as I have done for you, you should also do."

PUTTING PRAYER INTO PRACTICE

Christ washed even the feet of Judas! No one is undeserving of your attention or your service. This is not the philosophy, however, of the current culture. Catch yourself today when you resist giving someone your time or compassion.

PRAYER

May my prayer continue
in service to others,
for where I spend my time
is where I spend my heart.

CANTICLE Canticle of St. Patrick

Evening Prayer

Begin with page 179.

SCRIPTURE John 13:14

If I, therefore, the master and teacher, have washed your feet, you ought to wash one another's feet.

REFLECTION

Is where I spend my time consistent with my personal priorities and with gospel values?

PRAYER

You, who have the power
to command sun and stars,
kneel to wash my feet?
My God! How can I return such love?

CANTICLE Canticle of Zechariah

Opening Song for Morning Prayer

SALUTATION Hosea 6:3a

Let us know, let us strive to know the LORD; as certain as the dawn is his coming, and his judgment shines forth like the light of day!

SONG Psalm 91:1-7

You who dwell in the shelter of the Most High,
    who abide in the shadow of the Almighty,
Say to the LORD, "My refuge and my fortress,
    my God, in whom I trust."
For he will rescue you from the snare of the fowler,
    from the destroying pestilence.
With his pinions he will cover you,
    and under his wings you shall take refuge;
his faithfulness is a buckler and a shield.
You shall not fear the terror of the night
    nor the arrow that flies by day;
Not the pestilence that roams in darkness
    nor the devastating plague at noon.
Though a thousand fall at your side,
    ten thousand at your right side,
    near you it shall not come.

Turn to the page with today's date for the continuation of Morning Prayer.

Opening Song for Evening Prayer

SALUTATION

Your light, Lord,
overcomes the darkness.

SONG Psalm 91:8-16

Rather with your eyes shall you behold
    and see the requital of the wicked,
Because you have the LORD for your refuge;
    you have made the Most High your stronghold.
No evil shall befall you,
    nor shall affliction come near your tent,
For to his angels he has given command about you,
    that they guard you in all your ways.
Upon their hands they shall bear you up,
    lest you dash your foot against a stone.
You shall tread upon the asp and the viper;
    you shall trample down the lion and the dragon.

Because he clings to me, I will deliver him;
    I set him on high because he acknowledges my name.
He shall call upon me and I will answer him;
    I will be with him in distress;
I will deliver him and glorify him;
    with length of days I will gratify him
    and will show him my salvation.

Turn to the page with today's date for the continuation of Evening Prayer.

Morning Prayer

Begin with page 194.

SCRIPTURE 1 Corinthians 3:18-20

Let no one deceive himself. If anyone among you considers himself wise in this age, let him become a fool so as to become wise. For the wisdom of this world is foolishness in the eyes of God, for it is written:

"He catches the wise in their own ruses,"

and again:

"The Lord knows the thoughts of the wise, that they are vain."

WORDS OF WISDOM

In Leo Tolstoy's "The Death of Ivan Ilych," the main character, a lawyer in his forties, buys a house. In the course of fixing it up, Ivan falls from a ladder and seriously injures himself. As this accident mysteriously leads him to his death, he gradually becomes aware of the emptiness of life.

As family and friends learn of his terminal illness and, one by one, recoil in fear and embarrassment, Ivan makes a new discovery: "In them he saw himself, all in which he had lived—and saw clearly that it was not the right thing; it was a horrible, vast deception that concealed both life and death."

PRAYER

> To look at the world
> on the world's terms
> is indeed distressing.
> It is only when I see myself
> as a child of your love, God,
> that deceptions vanish
> and life here and now
> takes on meaning.

CANTICLE Wisdom Canticle

Evening Prayer

Begin with page 195.

SCRIPTURE *See page 196.*

REFLECTION

In what ways do I deceive myself?

PRAYER

> By your cross and resurrection
> you have saved the world.

CANTICLE Canticle of Mary

Morning Prayer

Begin with page 194.

SCRIPTURE Luke 23:28b-29

Daughters of Jerusalem, do not weep for me; weep instead for yourselves and for your children, for indeed, the days are coming when people will say, "Blessed are the barren, the wombs that never bore and the breasts that never nursed."

WORDS OF WISDOM

How we deal with death, of course, is tied in with how we respond to all the little deaths in our lives—the loss of friends, family, lovers, of particularly special times and places, of jobs or opportunities, hopes and dreams, or belief systems. What is interesting to me is that it does not seem necessary for many people to suffer in large ways if they learn the small, daily ways of giving to others and of letting go of the present to meet the unknown. Some people need to face "the worst" to learn this lesson. Other people do not. The dailyness of giving and letting go gives them the skills they need to cope when a loved one dies or they find themselves critically ill.[3]

PRAYER

> Help me to die a little each day
> so that the final break
> from the earthly world
> to the spiritual one
> is but a small step.

CANTICLE Canticle of Judith

Evening Prayer

Begin with page 195.

SCRIPTURE *See page 198.*

REFLECTION

In what ways am I unwilling to let go, on a daily basis, of people, things, habits, attitudes, expectations?

PRAYER

> I adore you, O Christ,
> and I bless you,
> because by your holy cross
> you have redeemed the world.

CANTICLE Canticle of St. Francis

Morning Prayer

Begin with page 194.

SCRIPTURE John 11:43b-44

[Jesus] cried out in a loud voice, "Lazarus, come out!"
The dead man came out, tied hand and foot with burial
bands, and his face was wrapped in a cloth. So Jesus said
to them, "Untie him and let him go."

COMMENTARY

We have built our own tombs, raising walls of selfishness
around us. Jesus calls us out into the light.

PRAYER

Today, Lord,
as I see you in everyone I meet,
awaken me from my sleep of selfishness
so that I may come alive
to your presence in my life.

CANTICLE Canticle of St. Patrick

Evening Prayer

Begin with page 195.

SCRIPTURE *See page 200.*

REFLECTION

In what ways has my selfishness kept me from loving?

PRAYER

For calling my name
and offering to heal me
and restore me with new life,
I thank you, Divine Healer.

CANTICLE Canticle of Zechariah

Morning Prayer

Begin with page 194.

SCRIPTURE Jeremiah 7:23b-24

Listen to my voice; then I will be your God and you shall be my people. Walk in all the ways that I command you, so that you may prosper.

But they obeyed not, nor did they pay heed. They walked in the hardness of their evil hearts and turned their backs, not their faces, to me.

COMMENTARY

How many times do we fail to be prophets? To be a prophet is to live a life of integrity and commitment. How often do we fail to live up to our promises?

PRAYER

Brother Jesus,
keep me from choosing comfort over commitment.
Sometimes I do not listen to your voice
because I want to indulge my emotions,
my anger, pride, jealousy and lust.
I want to satisfy my greed for power or possessions.
Save me from my slavery to selfishness.

CANTICLE Wisdom Canticle

Evening Prayer

Begin with page 195.

SCRIPTURE *See page 202.*

REFLECTION Have you ever thought of yourself as a prophet? If yes, why? If no, why not?

PRAYER

Divine Essence,
you who are the Word-made-flesh,
show me my becoming.
Empower me with the knowledge of my potential
so that I may, in awe, unfold in trust and faith.

Glory be to the Father....

CANTICLE Canticle of Mary

Morning Prayer

Begin with page 194.

SCRIPTURE John 8:12b

> I am the light of the world. Whoever follows me will not walk in darkness, but will have the light of life.

PUTTING PRAYER INTO PRACTICE

God is the light and we are like stained glass windows. If we stand in the light, our lives are bright, full of color and interesting. That doesn't mean we are doing extraordinary things like starting a mission or performing miracles. It does mean that whatever we are doing takes on color and shine. For instance, the clerk in the store who is cheerful, courteous and helpful brightens the lives of the customers much more than the snippy clerk who can't wait until quitting time. If your life is full of color and light, celebrate. If it could use a little brightening, remember that you yourself are a vessel of divine light, so today look for ways to make that extra effort to shine.

PRAYER

In the radiance of your love,
I stand transformed.
Still my restless spirit, Lord,
you who are infinite light,
so that I may reflect your rays
in the world around me.

CANTICLE Canticle of St. Patrick

Evening Prayer

Begin with page 195.

SCRIPTURE *See page 204.*

REFLECTION Does my life reflect the Good News?

PRAYER

> The sun is not in sight yet
> but I am at peace
> with the knowledge
> of the promise of dawn.
>
> Glory be to the Father....

CANTICLE Canticle of St. Francis

Morning Prayer

Begin with page 194.

SCRIPTURE Luke 16:19-21

There was a rich man who dressed in purple garments and fine linen and dined sumptuously each day. And lying at his door was a poor man named Lazarus, covered with sores, who would gladly have eaten his fill of the scraps that fell from the rich man's table.

PUTTING PRAYER INTO PRACTICE

How are you like the rich man? What person or group of people do you ignore? As you make your rounds today, discover at least one "Lazarus" in your life.

PRAYER

All around me are opportunities
to say a kind word
and listen to a troubled heart.
But there are risks.
If I begin, where will it end?
Free me from my fear, Lord,
so that I am not blinded
to the needs around me.

CANTICLE Canticle of Mary

Evening Prayer

Begin with page 195.

SCRIPTURE Luke 16:25

Abraham replied [to the rich man], "My child, remember that you received what was good during your lifetime while Lazarus likewise received what was bad; but now he is comforted here, whereas you are tormented."

REFLECTION

Did I see with the eyes of God today and reach out to help with the hands and compassion of Christ?

PRAYER

For the riches you bestow upon me,
I am thankful
and in gratitude
I will pass them on.

CANTICLE Canticle of Judith

Morning Prayer

Begin with page 194.

SCRIPTURE Hosea 6:1a

Come, let us return to the LORD....

COMMENTARY

Prayer is not a technique but a simple yearning for God.
God embraces us in the silence and solitude of
prayer—not so much to delight or protect us as to give
us the divine strength and love so that we may grow
toward wholeness and share God's strength and love
with others.

PRAYER

Come to me, Lord,
or, rather,
let me come to you.
For you are already
the essence of my being,
but I am often unaware of
your invisible presence.

CANTICLE Canticle of Mary

Evening Prayer

Begin with page 195.

SCRIPTURE Hosea 6:1a

Come, let us return to the LORD....

REFLECTION

In what ways do I need to return to the Lord?

PRAYER

You are my source;
my soul finds solace in you.
Embrace me now,
God and Creator,
as I sit in silent stillness.

Sit "in silent stillness" for several minutes and wait for the Lord's embrace.

CANTICLE Canticle of Zechariah

Morning Prayer

Begin with page 194.

SCRIPTURE John 8:23b-24

You belong to what is below, I belong to what is above. You belong to this world, but I do not belong to this world. That is why I told you that you will die in your sins. For if you do not believe that I AM, you will die in your sins.

COMMENTARY

Jesus brings us a glimpse of the world above—the higher part of our nature. Without an understanding of our divine nobility, we would live like the animals.

PRAYER

You give me dignity;
you show me personhood.
Proudly I proclaim
my divine ancestry!

Glory be to the Father....

CANTICLE Canticle of Zechariah

Evening Prayer

Begin with page 195.

SCRIPTURE John 8:24b

For if you do not believe that I AM, you will die in your sins.

REFLECTION

At what times in my life have I felt in tune with my higher nature?

Write the circumstances surrounding these times in your spiritual journal, if you are keeping one.

PRAYER

Even in the darkness of the night,
I do not fear.
For you, Christ,
show me the way.

CANTICLE Wisdom Canticle

Morning Prayer

Begin with page 194.

SCRIPTURE John 8:31b-32, 34-35

If you remain in my word, you will truly be my disciples,
and you will know the truth, and the truth will set you
free.... Amen, amen, I say to you, everyone who commits
sin is a slave of sin. A slave does not remain in a
household forever, but a son always remains.

COMMENTARY

Christ's message cuts the strings on our slave-like
existence. He calls us to full personhood—sons and
daughters of God. When the focus and meaning of our
lives becomes love, we are flooded with a sense of
purpose, strength and fulfillment. Be alert today for the
times when you begin to think negatively toward
someone and harbor hate. Notice what those thoughts
do to your body and your attitude compared to thoughts
of openness and generosity.

PRAYER

How wonderful is the message you bring,
Divine Counselor, to me and to all your children,
who are eager to break the bonds
of passion and hate.

CANTICLE Canticle of St. Patrick

Evening Prayer

Begin with page 195.

SCRIPTURE John 8:32b

...[T]he truth will set you free.

REFLECTION

At what times during the day did I feel free and whole?

PRAYER

You have set us free,
Wonderful Counselor,
and given us the keys to the Kingdom.
Unworthy child that I am,
I rest in your mansion.

Our Father....

CANTICLE Canticle of Judith

Morning Prayer

Begin with page 194.

SCRIPTURE Ephesians 5:8-12

For you were once darkness, but now you are light in the Lord. Live as children of light, for light produces every kind of goodness and righteousness and truth. Try to learn what is pleasing to the Lord. Take no part in the fruitless works of darkness; rather expose them, for it is shameful even to mention the things done by them in secret....

PUTTING PRAYER INTO PRACTICE

Do you have any secrets? Twelve-step programs insist that we are as sick as our secrets. Wherever there is secretiveness there is usually sin and shame. Today bring one secret to the light.

PRAYER

Uncover my shame
with your forgiving love.
Lord, lead me to the light.
Heal my secret wounds.

CANTICLE Canticle of Mary

Evening Prayer

Begin with page 195.

SCRIPTURE Ephesians 5:9

...[L]ight produces every kind of goodness and righteousness and truth.

REFLECTION

I am blind when I am not in touch with my dark side. Did I let the Lord's light shine on my darkness today?

PRAYER

In the shelter of your arms, Lord,
I rest in the peace and calm
of the coming night.

CANTICLE Canticle of Zechariah

Notes

[1] Excerpt from *The Vision of the Past* by Pierre Teilhard de Chardin, copyright ©1967 by Harper and Row, is used by permission of Georges Borchardt, Inc.

[2] Excerpt from *The Story of My Life*, by Helen Keller, copyright ©1903, 1954, 1961, 1988 is used with the permission of New American Library.

[3] Excerpt from *The Hero Within*, copyright © 1986 by Carol S. Pearson, is reprinted with the permission of the publisher, HarperSanFrancisco.

April

Opening Song for Morning Prayer

SALUTATION

> He will come to us like the rain,
> like spring rain that waters the earth.

SONG Psalm 29:1-4

> Give to the LORD, you sons of God,
>   give to the LORD glory and praise,
> Give to the LORD the glory due his name;
>   adore the LORD in holy attire.

> The voice of the LORD is over the waters,
>   the God of glory thunders,
>   the LORD, over vast waters.
> The voice of the LORD is mighty;
>   the voice of the LORD is majestic.

Turn to the page with today's date for the continuation of Morning Prayer.

Opening Song for Evening Prayer

SALUTATION

Almighty Artist,
you who paint the sky with splendid sunsets,
give me the grace
to see your design in all of creation.

SONG Psalm 29:7-11

The voice of the LORD strikes fiery flames;
    the voice of the LORD shakes the desert,
    the LORD shakes the wilderness of Kadesh.
The voice of the LORD twists the oaks
     and strips the forests,
    and in his temple all say, "Glory!"

The LORD is enthroned above the flood;
    the LORD is enthroned as king forever.
May the LORD give strength to his people;
    may the LORD bless his people with peace!

Turn to the page with today's date for the continuation of Evening Prayer.

Morning Prayer

Begin with page 218.

SCRIPTURE John :13b-14

Everyone who drinks this water will be thirsty again; but
whoever drinks the water I shall give will never thirst;
the water I shall give will become in him a spring of
water welling up to eternal life.

PUTTING PRAYER INTO PRACTICE

The flow of divine grace is established by the soul's
thirst. The greater the thirst, the more the soul opens
itself up to receive that divine flow. Get in touch with
your own thirst today. Don't substitute the waters of this
world for the springs of eternal life. Go without water for
as long as you can. Let your thirst be a reminder of your
dependence on God.

PRAYER

All you who are thirsty,
come to the water!
...Come, without paying and without cost,
drink wine and milk! (Isaiah 55:1a, c)

CANTICLE Wisdom Canticle

Evening Prayer

Begin with page 219.

SCRIPTURE John 4:14a

[W]hoever drinks the water I shall give will never thirst.

REFLECTION

Who is the Rainmaker? What would happen to my body if there were no water to nourish or cleanse it?

PRAYER

Lord and God, Divine Rainmaker,
you put out the fire
by quenching the thirst
of both body and soul.

CANTICLE Canticle of Judith

Morning Prayer

Begin with page 218.

SCRIPTURE John 8:51

Amen, Amen I say to you, whoever keeps my word will never see death.

WORDS OF WISDOM

We move closer to the truth only to the extent that we move further from life. What do we who love truth strive for in life? To be free of the body and of all evils that result from the life of the body. If this is so, then how can we fail to rejoice when death approaches? (Socrates, meeting with his friends just before his execution)

PRAYER

And so we can rejoice
when death approaches
because, when the body dies,
the spirit soars free.

CANTICLE Canticle of St. Francis

Evening Prayer

Begin with page 219.

SCRIPTURE *See page 222.*

REFLECTION

Death is a doorway to a new life.

PRAYER

For the gift of everlasting life,
I give thanks and praise.

Glory be to the Father....

CANTICLE Canticle of Zechariah

Morning Prayer

Begin with page 218.

SCRIPTURE Matthew 5:9

Blessed are the peacemakers,
for they will be called children of God.

COMMENTARY

To discover peace, a person must be, in a sense, in
solitude, for peace is the synthesizing of two opposite
views. To embrace a cause, a movement, a certain way of
thinking is to be one-sided and to join with that side. The
person who is a hermit in her/his heart must be
profoundly alone to discover the truth and to find peace
in the balance of opposing forces.

PRAYER

Reconciler of opposites,
Divine Trinity,
help me to discover that third side,
which unites opposites into one.

Glory be to the Father....

CANTICLE Canticle of St. Patrick

Evening Prayer

Begin with page 219.

SCRIPTURE *See page 224.*

REFLECTION

Do I recognize that in many circumstances there are several "right" ways?

PRAYER

For the mystery of the Trinity,
I now pray in thanksgiving and praise.

Glory be to the Father....

CANTICLE Wisdom Canticle

Morning Prayer

Begin with page 218.

SCRIPTURE John 14:6b

I am the way and the truth and the life.

SPIRITUAL EXERCISE

To allow this Scripture passage to take hold in you, close
your eyes and focus on the sensation of purity and light.
If it helps you, envision a field of snow with a winding
path, or picture yourself sitting in an area bathed in soft,
white light. The light is grace: Feel it penetrate your
body! Sit in the light of this grace.

PRAYER

As I bathe in your grace,
gentle God,
I am reminded
of the reason for my existence.
I return now to you,
who are my source.

CANTICLE Canticle of Zechariah

Evening Prayer

Begin with page 219.

SCRIPTURE John 14:6b

I am the way and the truth and the life.

REFLECTION

How often do I think of these words from Scripture when I choose the company I keep, the way I spend my time—both at work and play?

PRAYER

Unafraid, I go into the darkness,
for you, Christ, show me the way.

CANTICLE Wisdom Canticle

Morning Prayer

Begin with page 218.

SCRIPTURE John 8:50

I do not seek my own glory; there is one who seeks it and he is the one who judges.

MEDITATION

What a beautiful example Christ gives us here. And it is so simple to follow. Every time you make a decision or act, put it to this test: Are you seeking your own glory or God's?

Sit in silence now and meditate on putting this Scripture passage into practice in your daily schedule. Before you begin each day, think about the choices and paths you will be taking and choose the ways that lead to God's glory, rather than your own.

PRAYER

Be patient with me, Brother Jesus,
as I struggle to put your simple,
yet difficult,
teachings into practice.

CANTICLE Canticle of St. Patrick

Evening Prayer

Begin with page 219.

SCRIPTURE John 8:50

I do not seek my own glory; there is one who seeks it and he is the one who judges.

REFLECTION

What choices and actions did I make today that reflected God's glory?

PRAYER

Glory be to the Father....

CANTICLE Wisdom Canticle

Morning Prayer

Begin with page 218.

SCRIPTURE John 7:37-39a

On the last and greatest day of the feast, Jesus stood up and exclaimed, "Let anyone who thirsts come to me and drink. Whoever believes in me, as scripture says:

'Rivers of living water will flow from within him.' "

He said this in reference to the Spirit that those who came to believe in him were to receive.

PUTTING PRAYER INTO PRACTICE

Whenever you use water today, think of both its natural and its spiritual significance.

PRAYER

Christ, you call me to come to the well,
to the water that gives new life.
Here I am,
joyful and eager to absorb the flow
of your life-giving liquid.

CANTICLE Wisdom Canticle

Evening Prayer

Begin with page 219.

SCRIPTURE *See page 230.*

REFLECTION

In a way, water is like grace. Because it is abundant, I don't appreciate it.

PRAYER

May the showers of April
remind me of your gift of living waters,
Divine Rainmaker!

CANTICLE Canticle of St. Francis

Morning Prayer

Begin with page 218.

SCRIPTURE Isaiah 55:10-11

For just as from the heavens
the rain and snow come down
And do not return there
till they have watered the earth,
making it fertile and fruitful,
Giving seed to him who sows,
and bread to him who eats,
So shall my word be
that goes forth from my mouth;
It shall not return to me void,
but shall do my will,
achieving the end for which I sent it.

MEDITATION

Sit in stillness and silence. Imagine yourself being
bathed by divine love and understanding. Let the word of
God penetrate your mind and heart.

Silence

PRAYER

I drink of your goodness, God,
and am saturated by the source,
the essence of your being.

CANTICLE Canticle of Judith

Evening Prayer

Begin with page 219.

SCRIPTURE *See page 232.*

REFLECTION

In what ways did I live God's word today?

PRAYER

In the midst of conflict and stress,
your word brings comfort and calm.
Thank you, God.

CANTICLE Wisdom Canticle

Opening Song for Morning Prayer

SALUTATION Isaiah 50:4b-5

Morning after morning
   he opens my ear that I may hear;
And I have not rebelled,
   have not turned back.

SONG Psalm 51:3-4

Have mercy on me, O God, in your goodness;
   in the greatness of your compassion wipe out my
     offense.
Thoroughly wash me from my guilt
   and of my sin cleanse me.

Turn to the page with today's date for the continuation of Morning Prayer.

Opening Song for Evening Prayer

SALUTATION

> At twilight, I put my trust in you,
> steadfast God,
> to renew and revive my tired spirit.

SONG Psalm 51:5-10

> For I acknowledge my offense,
>   and my sin is before me always:
> "Against you only have I sinned,
>   and done what is evil in your sight"—
> That you may be justified in your sentence,
>   vindicated when you condemn.
> Indeed, in guilt was I born,
>   and in sin my mother conceived me;
> Behold, you are pleased with sincerity of heart,
>   and in my innermost being you teach me wisdom.
>
> Cleanse me of sin with hyssop, that I may be purified;
>   wash me, and I shall be whiter than snow.
> Let me hear the sounds of joy and gladness;
>   the bones you have crushed will rejoice.

Turn to the page with today's date for the continuation of Evening Prayer.

Morning Prayer

Begin with page 234.

SCRIPTURE Isaiah 50:7

> The Lord GOD is my help
> therefore I am not disgraced;
> I have set my face like flint,
> knowing that I shall not be put to shame.

PUTTING PRAYER INTO PRACTICE

Dare to be different! That is what Isaiah is telling us: Set your face like flint in the face of adversity. Be stubborn when it comes to personal ethics. Hold your ground in a humble, faith-filled way.

PRAYER

> Holy Spirit,
> fill me with the stamina
> to be steadfast in situations
> where others are taking action
> out of weakness and fear.
> Give me the strength
> to sow your love!

CANTICLE Canticle of St. Patrick

Evening Prayer

Begin with page 235.

SCRIPTURE *See page 236.*

REFLECTION

How often do I allow injustice to prevail out of laziness or concern for what others think?

PRAYER

As long as I am grounded in you, Lord,
I am blessed with a dignity
that shields me from shame.

CANTICLE Canticle of Mary

Morning Prayer

Begin with page 234.

SCRIPTURE John 8:47a

Whoever belongs to God hears the words of God....

PUTTING PRAYER INTO PRACTICE

The mind grows wise through reading, through the
exercise of logic and deduction. The heart grows wise
through experience. That is what prayer can be—an
experience of God. It is wisdom from another level, a
level that is not limited by intelligence or knowledge.
The pray-er who dares to dip into this level and run the
risk of intimacy with the Infinite will experience God and
a sense of communion with all the created.

PRAYER

Beyond petitions and repetitions
I come to you, Infinite One.
Silent and open I sit,
waiting for your word.

Silence

CANTICLE Canticle of Mary

Evening Prayer

Begin with page 235.

SCRIPTURE John 8:47a

Whoever belongs to God hears the words of God....

REFLECTION

Was I able to hear the Lord speak to me today?

PRAYER

You, who are life,
come upon me in the strangest places,
sowing solace and wisdom.

CANTICLE Wisdom Canticle

Morning Prayer

Begin with page 234.

SCRIPTURE Matthew 6:26a

Look at the birds in the sky; they do not sow or reap,
they gather nothing into barns, yet your heavenly Father
feeds them.

MEDITATION

If you were a baby bird and you had your choice of
growing up in the beautiful woods, seeking your own
food, or living in a lovely cage and being well fed, which
would you choose?

SILENT MEDITATION

CANTICLE Canticle of St. Francis

Evening Prayer

Begin with page 235.

SCRIPTURE *See page 240.*

REFLECTION

What kind of bird am I? Do I realize that my desire to be cared for in a cage restricts my freedom? Am I aware that the freedom of life in the woods has its risks? Have I resigned myself to the consequences that come with either decision?

PRAYER

For the freedom to make my own choices,
and the wisdom to choose wisely,
I thank you, Loving God.

CANTICLE Canticle of Mary

Morning Prayer

Begin with page 234.

SCRIPTURE John 8:28-29

So Jesus said [to them], "When you lift up the Son of Man, then you will realize that I AM, and that I do nothing on my own, but I say only what the Father taught me. The one who sent me is with me. He has not left me alone, because I always do what is pleasing to him."

COMMENTARY

Relationships bloom when the people involved please one another. So, too, your friendship with God. The more you try to understand what will please God, the more the feeling grows in you that God will not forsake you.

PRAYER

Today I will take the time
to consider what would please you,
loving God.

CANTICLE Canticle of St. Patrick

Evening Prayer

Begin with page 235.

SCRIPTURE John 8:29c

...[B]ecause I always do what is pleasing to him.

REFLECTION

In what ways did I try to please God today?

MEDITATION

Take a minute or two to sit quietly and meditate on all the things God has given you—the ways God has tried to please you.

CANTICLE Canticle of Mary

Morning Prayer

Begin with page 234.

SCRIPTURE John 20:19

On the evening of that first day of the week, when the doors were locked, where the disciples were, for fear of the Jews, Jesus came and stood in their midst and said to them, "Peace be with you."

PUTTING PRAYER INTO PRACTICE

Christ broke down the walls of fear to reach the disciples. As Christians, we too are called to destroy the barriers of fear and isolation that divide us.

PRAYER

Maker of miracles,
help me to remove my mask of pretense
and break through the barriers
that separate me from others.

CANTICLE Canticle of Zechariah

Evening Prayer

Begin with page 235.

SCRIPTURE *See page 244.*

REFLECTION

At what times in my life did I feel at one with a person, a group, the world or the Spirit?

PRAYER

You show us our at-one-ness,
God of all.
For these sacred moments of communion,
I thank you. Alleluia!

CANTICLE Canticle of St. Francis

Morning Prayer

Begin with page 234.

SCRIPTURE John 20:20-21

When he had said this, he showed them his hands and
his side. The disciples rejoiced when they saw the Lord.
[Jesus] said to them again, "Peace be with you. As the
Father has sent me, so I send you."

SPIRITUAL EXERCISE

Imagine yourself being crucified and deserted by most of
your friends. Imagine further what kind of love it would
take for you to say to the deserters, when you next saw
them, "Peace be with you."

Think now of the anger you are carrying and holding
against another (or others). Compare the wrong you
suffered to what Christ suffered. Allow his love to flood
your heart and wash away your hurt in forgiveness.

Sit in silence with this thought.

PRAYER

Compassionate Christ,
erase the hurt and anxiety from my heart,
so that I may enter into the peace
that surpasses understanding.

CANTICLE Canticle of Zechariah

Evening Prayer

Begin with page 235.

SCRIPTURE John 20:21a

[Jesus] said to them again, "Peace be with you."

REFLECTION

What price am I prepared to pay for peace?

PRAYER

Peace is the spoil
when love is the victor
in fierce, interior battle.

CANTICLE Canticle of Mary

Morning Prayer

Begin with page 234.

SCRIPTURE Psalm 51:12-13

> A clean heart create for me, O God,
>   and a steadfast spirit renew within me.
> Cast me not out from your presence,
>   and your holy spirit take not from me.

PUTTING PRAYER INTO PRACTICE

A clean heart is the result of a long process of cooperation with God. Today, when you don't feel good about something, take a moment to follow that feeling to its source. Chances are it will lead you to some impurity of heart, something you have done or thought that is selfish. Rejoice when you discover an area that you can "clean."

PRAYER

Giver of all good things, help me to remember
that a steadfast spirit proceeds from pure intentions
and pure intentions proceed from a clean heart.
Create a clean heart for me, O God.

CANTICLE Canticle of St. Patrick

Evening Prayer

Begin with page 235.

SCRIPTURE Psalm 51:12a

A clean heart create for me, O God.

REFLECTION

What are the qualities of a pure, clean heart?

PRAYER

You surround me with your love;
it pierces my heart.
I am lost in your divine grace.

CANTICLE Wisdom Canticle

Opening Song for Morning Prayer

SALUTATION

The sound of morning
is the song of creation
awakening to a new day.

SONG Psalm 72:1-6

O God, with your judgment endow the king,
and with your justice, the king's son;
He shall govern your people with justice
and your afflicted ones with judgment.
The mountains shall yield peace for the people,
and the hills justice.
He shall defend the afflicted among the people,
save the children of the poor,
and crush the oppressor.

May he endure as long as the sun,
and like the moon through all generations.
He shall be like rain coming down on the meadow,
like showers watering the earth.

*Turn to the page with today's date for the continuation of
Morning Prayer.*

Opening Song for Evening Prayer

SALUTATION

Stillness and calm
descend with the darkness.
In wondrous expectation,
I turn my thoughts to you, O Lord.

SONG Psalm 72:11-13, 17

All kings shall pay him homage;
    all nations shall serve him.

For he shall rescue the poor man when he cries out,
    and the afflicted when he has no one to help him.
He shall have pity for the lowly and the poor;
    the lives of the poor he shall save....

May his name be blessed forever;
    as long as the sun his name shall remain.
In him shall all the tribes of the earth be blessed;
    all the nations shall proclaim his happiness.

Turn to the page with today's date for the continuation of Evening Prayer.

Morning Prayer

Begin with page 250.

SCRIPTURE John 3:19-21

And this is the verdict, that the light came into the world, but people preferred darkness to light, because their works were evil. For everyone who does wicked things hates the light and does not come toward the light, so that his works might not be exposed. But whoever lives the truth comes to the light, so that his works may be clearly seen as done in God.

WORDS OF WISDOM

My deeds, whatever they may be, will be forgotten sooner or later, and I myself will be no more. Why, then, do anything? How can anyone fail to see this and live? That's what is amazing! It is possible to live only as long as life intoxicates us; once we are sober we cannot help seeing that it is all a delusion, a stupid delusion! (*Confession*, Leo Tolstoy)

PRAYER

O Creator of life,
as I let go of illusions
and begin to understand
the true nature of things,
deliver me from the temptation
to lose myself in disillusionment.

CANTICLE Canticle of Zechariah

Evening Prayer

Begin with page 251.

SCRIPTURE *See page 252.*

REFLECTION What do I do when I become discouraged or stressed?

PRAYER

That I may sit in sobriety, Lord,
quietly, content in my room,
without the compulsive need
for people, excitement, possessions or drugs:
This I pray.

CANTICLE Wisdom Canticle

Morning Prayer

Begin with page 250.

SCRIPTURE Matthew 5:10

Blessed are they who are persecuted
   for the sake of righteousness,
   for theirs is the kingdom of Heaven.

PUTTING PRAYER INTO PRACTICE

Violence is a cycle. A person receiving a hurt passes it on
to another, and so it goes from person to person and
generation to generation. This is especially evident today
in the cycle of abuse within families. Christ stopped the
cycle. That is one of the signs of the cross: stopping the
cycle of violence and absorbing it rather than passing it
on. Think about that today when you feel hurt or angry;
resist the temptation to dump it on another.

CANTICLE Canticle of St. Patrick

Evening Prayer

Begin with page 251.

SCRIPTURE *See page 254.*

REFLECTION Did I show love to those who offended me?

PRAYER

Lamb of God,
you willingly took upon yourself
the pain of the world.

Glory be to the Father....

CANTICLE Canticle of Zechariah

Morning Prayer

Begin with page 250.

SCRIPTURE Ezekiel 47:1ab, 9, 12

Then he brought me back to the entrance of the temple,
and I saw water flowing out from beneath the threshold
of the temple towards the east.... "Wherever the river
flows, every sort of living creature that can multiply shall
live, and there shall be abundant fish, for wherever this
water comes, the sea shall be made fresh.... Along both
banks of the river, fruit trees of every kind shall grow;
their leaves shall not fade, nor their fruit fail. Every
month they shall bear fresh fruit, for they shall be
watered by the flow from the sanctuary. Their fruit shall
serve for food, and their leaves for medicine."

COMMENTARY

Water is used as a sacred symbol for healing several
times throughout Scripture.

PRAYER

May I grow in watchfulness,
Creator of heaven and earth,
careful not to waste your divine gift
that falls from the heavens
and springs from the earth.

CANTICLE Canticle of Judith

Evening Prayer

Begin with page 251.

SCRIPTURE *See page 256.*

REFLECTION

How is water a healing symbol for me?

PRAYER

Giver of all good things,
I am grateful for the gift of water,
which heals, purifies and energizes.

CANTICLE Canticle of St. Francis

Morning Prayer

Begin with page 250.

SCRIPTURE Matthew 5:7

> Blessed are the merciful,
>   for they will be shown mercy.

PUTTING PRAYER INTO PRACTICE

Probably the reason most of the saints are so forgiving and merciful is that they are in touch with their own selfishness. The more aware you become of your own need for forgiveness, the more you become forgiving of others. When someone irritates you today, stop and think of all the times you have irritated another.

PRAYER

> Help me to be humble, Lord,
> so that I may see my faults.
> Give me the strength
> to search out my shadow side,
> so that another's darkness
> does not overcome me.

CANTICLE Canticle of St. Patrick

Evening Prayer

Begin with page 251.

SCRIPTURE Matthew 5:7

Blessed are the merciful,
for they will be shown mercy.

REFLECTION

Was I aware, today, of the times I offended another?

PRAYER

Lord, I remember
all that has been forgiven me.
Your mercy abounds!
Your love is everlasting!

Our Father....

CANTICLE Canticle of Judith

Morning Prayer

Begin with page 250.

SCRIPTURE Ezekiel 31:3-5, 10-11

Behold a cypress [cedar] in Lebanon,
  beautiful of branch, lofty of stature,
  amid the very clouds lifted its crest.
Waters made it grow, the abyss made it flourish,
  sending its waters round where it was planted,
  turning its streams to all the trees of the field.
Thus it grew taller than every other tree of the field
  and longer of branch because of the abundant water.

Therefore thus says the Lord GOD: Because it became
lofty in stature, raising its crest among the clouds, and
because it became proud in heart at its height, I have
handed it over to the mightiest of the nations, which has
dealt with it in keeping with its wickedness. I humiliated
it.

WORDS OF WISDOM

It cannot be doubted that the poor can more easily attain
the blessing of humility than those who are rich. In the
case of the poor, the lack of worldly goods is often
accompanied by a quiet gentleness, whereas the rich are
more prone to arrogance. Nevertheless, many wealthy
people are disposed to use their abundance not to swell
their own pride but to perform works of benevolence.
They consider their greatest gain what they spend to
alleviate the distress of others.

This virtue is open to all men, no matter what their class or condition, because all can be equal in their willingness to give, however unequal they may be in earthly fortune. (St. Leo the Great)[1]

PRAYER

Let me seek a simple life, Lord,
full of gentleness and generosity,
where I may gain peace
through the virtue of sharing.

CANTICLE Canticle of Zechariah

Evening Prayer

Begin with page 251.

SCRIPTURE *See page 260.*

REFLECTION In what ways am I arrogant?

PRAYER

You share your wealth with me,
O King who lived in poverty.
You share your life with me,
O crucified Lord.
I give you thanks.

CANTICLE Canticle of Mary

Morning Prayer

Begin with page 250.

SCRIPTURE John 6:32-33, 35b

So Jesus said to them, "Amen, amen, I say to you, it was not Moses who gave the bread from heaven; my Father gives you the true bread from heaven. For the bread of God is that which comes down from heaven and gives life to the world....

"I am the bread of life; whoever comes to me will never hunger, and whoever believes in me will never thirst."

PUTTING PRAYER INTO PRACTICE

Whatever nourishes us is our "bread." A loaf of bread satisfies our stomach, but the human psyche hungers for communion with the Creator. One way to get in touch with the Creator is to get in touch with your own creativity.

PRAYER

Shaper of the cosmos,
you give color and drama to my life.
My soul cries out for creative expression;
it dreams and designs a response to the divine.

CANTICLE Wisdom Canticle

Evening Prayer

Begin with page 251.

SCRIPTURE *See page 262.*

REFLECTION

What is "bread" to me? What sustains and nourishes my life?

PRAYER

Move me from the material realm,
Brother Jesus,
so I may fall at your feet.
For the bread you give
is everlasting.

CANTICLE Canticle of St. Francis

Morning Prayer

Begin with page 250.

SCRIPTURE John 3:16-17

For God so loved the world that he gave his only Son, so that everyone who believes in him might not perish but might have eternal life. For God did not send his Son into the world to condemn the world, but that the world might be saved through him.

WORDS OF WISDOM

Ah, you know it yourself, Lord, through having borne the anguish of it as a man: on certain days the world seems a terrifying thing: huge, blind and brutal. It buffets us about, drags us along, and kills us with complete indifference....

[T]hat I may not succumb to the temptation to curse the universe and him who made it, teach me to adore it by seeing you concealed within it....

We have only to believe. And the more threatening and irreducible reality appears, the more firmly and desperately must we believe. Then, little by little, we shall see the universal horror unbend, and then smile upon us, and then take us in its more than human arms. (Pierre Teilhard de Chardin)[2]

CANTICLE Canticle of Mary

Evening Prayer

Begin with page 251.

SCRIPTURE *See page 264.*

MEDITATION

Imagine yourself sitting at the feet of Jesus. What would he tell you about loving your spouse, children, parents, close friends? Sit quietly and listen.

PRAYER

You created the world in love.
Help me, one of your creations,
to manifest that love.

Glory be to the Father....

CANTICLE Wisdom Canticle

Opening Song for Morning Prayer

SALUTATION

As you banish the dark from the dawn,
Lord of the Morning,
enlighten my thoughts and actions
as I move through my day.

SONG Psalm 98:1-4

Sing to the LORD a new song,
    for he has done wondrous deeds;
His right hand has won victory for him,
    his holy arm.
The LORD has made his salvation known:
    in the sight of the nations he has revealed his justice.
He has remembered his kindness and his faithfulness
    toward the house of Israel.
All the ends of the earth have seen
    the salvation by our God.

Sing joyfully to the LORD, all you lands;
    break into song; sing praise.

Turn to the page with today's date for the continuation of Morning Prayer.

Opening Song for Evening Prayer

SALUTATION

As I put the rigors of the day to rest,
loving Father/Mother,
I find comfort and peace
in the shadow of your wing.

SONG Psalm 98:4-9

Sing joyfully to the LORD, all you lands;
   break into song; sing praise.
Sing praise to the LORD with the harp,
   with the harp and melodious song.
With trumpets and the sound of the horn
   sing joyfully before the King, the LORD.

Let the sea and what fills it resound,
   the world and those who dwell in it;
Let the rivers clap their hands,
   the mountains shout with them for joy
Before the LORD, for he comes,
   for he comes to rule the earth;
He will rule the world with justice
   and the peoples with equity.

Turn to the page with today's date for the continuation of Evening Prayer.

Morning Prayer

Begin with page 266.

SCRIPTURE 1 Corinthians 4:9-10a

> For as I see it, God has exhibited us apostles as the last of all, like people sentenced to death, since we have become a spectacle to the world, to angels and human beings alike. We are fools on Christ's account....

WORDS OF WISDOM

> "I feel like making a placard to wear on the front and back of me," said a parish priest one morning at Mass. "It would read, 'I am God's Fool' on the front side and on the back it would read 'Whose fool are you?' "

> Most of us make fools of ourselves for money, power, attention, status, romantic love and so on, but seldom take risks that appear foolish to the world for God. Do something today for God that is risky—something that might risk your cool.

PRAYER

> Sometimes those who trust in you, Lord,
> are looked upon as fools by the world.
> But material treasures are temporary
> and relying on them is the real folly!

CANTICLE Canticle of Zechariah

Evening Prayer

Begin with page 267.

SCRIPTURE *See page 268.*

REFLECTION

In what ways does my concern about appearing foolish
limit my response to Christ's invitation?

PRAYER

You are always there,
waiting with the true treasure,
my Lord and my God.

Glory be to the Father....

CANTICLE Wisdom Canticle

Morning Prayer

Begin with page 266.

SCRIPTURE Matthew 5:3

Blessed are the poor in spirit,
for theirs is the kingdom of heaven.

COMMENTARY

Blessed are those who realize that all they have, even
those things obtained through hard work, is a gift. No
matter how much worldly security we possess, we are
dependent on God for our happiness, health and life.
When you feel cocky or independent, remember this
Beatitude and be grateful.

LITANY OF GRATITUDE

For this land of liberty in which I live,
Lord, I am truly grateful.

For the ability to see, hear and walk,
Lord, I am truly grateful.

For the gift of life, both material and spiritual,
Lord, I am truly grateful.

For the beauty of nature—
trees, flowers, sunsets and waterfalls—
Lord, I am truly grateful.

For the people you place in my life,
Lord, I am truly grateful.

For my daily bread,
Lord, I am truly grateful.

For my faith in you
and the grace you give to sustain it,
Lord, I am truly grateful.

CANTICLE Canticle of St. Patrick

Evening Prayer

Begin with page 267.

SCRIPTURE *See page 270.*

REFLECTION

How much of the "good life" do I take for granted?

PRAYER

Pray again the Litany of Gratitude. Add some verses of
your own.

CANTICLE Canticle of St. Francis

Morning Prayer

Begin with page 266.

SCRIPTURE John 6:51

I am the living bread that came down from heaven;
whoever eats this bread will live forever; and the bread
that I will give is my flesh for the life of the world.

PUTTING PRAYER INTO PRACTICE

The hunger for friendship and love is almost as basic as
the hunger for physical food. In this way, let me be food
for another today.

PRAYER

Father God,
you sent manna from heaven.
Christ the Son,
you gave us your flesh and blood.
Holy Spirit,
as I consume the divine essence
let me, in turn, be consumed
as bread for my brothers and sisters.

CANTICLE Canticle of St. Patrick

Evening Prayer

Begin with page 267.

SCRIPTURE *See page 272.*

REFLECTION

How am I bread for another?

PRAYER

Your nourishing merciful love surrounds me,
Brother Jesus.
I need only to breathe in your goodness.

CANTICLE Canticle of Judith

Morning Prayer

Begin with page 266.

SCRIPTURE Luke 24:13-15, 30-31

Now that very day two of them were going to a village seven miles from Jerusalem called Emmaus, and they were conversing about all the things that had occurred. And it happened that while they were conversing and debating, Jesus himself drew near and walked with them....

And it happened that, while he was with them at table, he took bread, said the blessing, broke it, and gave it to them. With that their eyes were opened and they recognized him, but he vanished from their sight.

COMMENTARY

Whenever we enter into a spirit-filled conversation, the Spirit of Jesus is present. Likewise with the breaking of the bread—for it is when we sit at the table in peace with one another that we can then recognize Christ in our fellow human beings.

PRAYER

Christ, you are within me
and within everyone I meet.
Help me to remember this as I converse
and break bread with my brothers and sisters.

CANTICLE Canticle of St. Patrick

Evening Prayer

Begin with page 267.

SCRIPTURE Luke 24:31b

...[A]nd they recognized him.

REFLECTION

Do I ever recognize Christ's spirit in myself, my actions or my attitudes?

Record these times in your spiritual journal, if you are keeping one.

PRAYER

Brother Jesus,
you share your strength.
You spill yourself out for me.
All honor and glory is yours!

CANTICLE Canticle of Mary

Morning Prayer

Begin with page 266.

SCRIPTURE Luke 24:32, 35

Then they said to each other, "Were not our hearts burning [within us] while he spoke to us on the way and opened the scriptures to us?" ...Then the two recounted what had taken place on the way and how he was made known to them in the breaking of the bread.

MEDITATION

Christ has disappeared from our sight, but it is our mission to make his presence known in the world.

The word *Mass* means "mission." Mass consists of four parts: gathering, Scripture, Eucharist and dismissal. The first three parts have already been accomplished when we leave church. It is up to us to continue the Mass—to renew Christ's presence in the world.

Meditate on the ways God may be calling you to do this.

PRAYER

Loving God,
show me the way
in my workplace,
in the market
and at home
to bring Christ's presence
(the power of love)
to those I meet.

CANTICLE Canticle of St. Patrick

Evening Prayer

Begin with page 267.

SCRIPTURE Luke 24:32b

Were not our hearts burning [within us] while he spoke to us on the way and opened the scriptures to us?

REFLECTION

How often does my heart burn with zeal for God's word?

CLOSING

Sit in silence for a few minutes and focus on all the beauty inside of you. End your silence with a short prayer of thanksgiving.

Morning Prayer

Begin with page 266.

SCRIPTURE Ezekiel 36:25-26

I will sprinkle clean water upon you to cleanse you from all your impurities, and from all your idols I will cleanse you. I will give you a new heart and place a new spirit within you, taking from your bodies your stony hearts and giving you natural hearts.

PUTTING PRAYER INTO PRACTICE

A new or "natural" heart softens one's outlook. It is a heart that looks upon the world with love rather than judgment. It is the heart that is unafraid to say no when no is the more loving— although difficult—answer. In your relations with others today, strive to use your natural heart.

PRAYER

Soften my heart, Yahweh,
and place your Spirit within me.

CANTICLE Canticle of Mary

Evening Prayer

Begin with page 267.

SCRIPTURE *See page 278.*

REFLECTION

In what ways today did I respond in love? In what ways today did I respond in fear?

PRAYER

Sometimes my heart is heavy
with the burdens of others.
But I draw strength
from the knowledge
that at those times
you will carry me,
Compassionate Creator!

CANTICLE Canticle of Judith

Morning Prayer

Begin with page 266.

SCRIPTURE Luke 24:39-43

"Look at my hands and feet, that it is I myself. Touch me and see, because a ghost does not have flesh and bones as you can see I have." And as he said this, he showed them his hands and his feet. While they were still incredulous for joy and were amazed, he asked them, "Have you anything here to eat?" They gave him a piece of baked fish; he took it and ate it in front of them.

PUTTING PRAYER INTO PRACTICE

The risen Christ seems to be inviting us to touch him and bring him into every aspect of our lives. Our God is not an awesome, frightening judge, but a tender, loving friend.

PRAYER

Maranatha! Come, Christ,
into the fiber of my being,
into my every act and word.

CANTICLE Canticle of St. Patrick

Evening Prayer

Begin with page 267.

SCRIPTURE *See page 280.*

REFLECTION

Am I afraid of God? Does my fear interfere with my love for God and for others?

PRAYER

Brother Jesus,
you touch and hold me
in the midst of gloom.
Your love is unfailing.
I am humbled by your mercy!

CANTICLE Canticle of Zechariah

Morning Prayer

Begin with page 266.

SCRIPTURE 1 John 1:5b-7a

> God is light and in him there is no darkness at all. If we
> say, "We have fellowship with him," while we continue to
> walk in darkness, we lie and do not act in truth. But if we
> walk in the light as he is in the light, then we have
> fellowship with one another....

PUTTING PRAYER INTO PRACTICE

> As the story goes, St. Catherine of Siena, a fourteenth-
> century mystic, would often ask God to put on her soul
> the weight (or punishment) of another's sins. She even
> did this for a common criminal on his way to the gallows.
> How great her love for her neighbor must have been!

PRAYER

> Lord of Light,
> when I walk in darkness
> I cause others to fall.
> But when I am enlightened,
> all who are around me can see.

CANTICLE Canticle of St. Patrick

Evening Prayer

Begin with page 267.

SCRIPTURE *See page 282.*

REFLECTION

Imagine the love required to take on the punishment for another's sins.

PRAYER

Come, darkness,
I do not fear your depth
or shudder at your mystery,
for the Lord lights my way.

CANTICLE Canticle of St. Francis

Morning Prayer

Begin with page 266.

SCRIPTURE John 14:12-14

Amen, amen, I say to you, whoever believes in me will do the works that I do, and will do greater ones than these, because I am going to the Father. And whatever you ask in my name, I will do, so that the Father may be glorified in the Son. If you ask anything of me in my name, I will do it.

PUTTING PRAYER INTO PRACTICE

Imagine the heritage Jesus has left you. You can do even greater things than he: Whatever you ask in his name, he will do. When you see suffering today, imagine what Christ would do in that situation. Then do it!

PRAYER

Lord, open my Christ-consciousness
to do your works and your will
whenever and wherever I find wounds
that need your healing graces.

CANTICLE Canticle of St. Patrick

Evening Prayer

Begin with page 267.

SCRIPTURE John 14:14

If you ask anything of me in my name, I will do it.

REFLECTION

In what ways did I comfort and heal today? When I looked upon suffering today, did I take the time to ask God for divine guidance?

PRAYER

You give me your power
to build your kingdom
here on earth.
But I become absorbed
in my own needs.
I am grateful for the grace you give me
to keep trying.

CANTICLE Wisdom Canticle

Notes

[1] Excerpt from *The Liturgy of the Hours*, copyright © 1974, International Commission on English in the Liturgy, Inc. All rights reserved.

[2] Excerpt from *The Divine Milieu*, by Pierre Teilhard de Chardin, English translation copyright © 1960 by William Collins Sons, Ltd., and Harper and Row, is reprinted with permission of Harper Collins Publishers.

May

Opening Song for Morning Prayer

SALUTATION

I lift my face
to the radiance of a new day
and ask blessings from the Lord of life!

SONG Psalm 42:2-5

As the hind longs for the running waters,
 so my soul longs for you, O God.
Athirst is my soul for God, the living God.
 When shall I go and behold the face of God?
My tears are my food day and night,
 as they say to me day after day,
 "Where is your God?"
Those times I recall,
 now that I pour out my soul within me,
When I went with the throng
 and led them in procession to the house of God,
Amid loud cries of joy and thanksgiving,
 with the multitude keeping festival.

*Turn to the page with today's date for the continuation of
Morning Prayer.*

Opening Song for Evening Prayer

SALUTATION

Weary and burdened,
I come to you in prayer.
Lord, comfort my troubled heart
and calm my anxious soul.

SONG Psalm 43:6

Why are you so downcast, O my soul?
Why do you sigh within me?
Hope in God! For I shall again be thanking him,
in the presence of my savior and my God.

Turn to the page with today's date for the continuation of Evening Prayer.

Morning Prayer

Begin with page 288.

SCRIPTURE Matthew 1:24

When Joseph awoke [from his dream], he did as the angel of the Lord had commanded him and took his wife into his home.

PUTTING PRAYER INTO PRACTICE

In today's world, the theology of risk has been replaced by the theology of blessed assurance or insurance. How wonderful, then, to reflect on the response of Joseph, who was told in a dream that the baby Mary carried was conceived through the Holy Spirit and sent to save humankind. St. Joseph risked his reputation, his livelihood, even his life, because he believed his dream was real and he dared to live it out.

Take advantage of opportunities today to love your neighbor—even when it means taking a risk.

PRAYER

Make me aware, Creator God,
of the times I fail
to love my neighbor as myself
because I am unwilling
to take a risk.

CANTICLE Canticle of St. Patrick

Evening Prayer

Begin with page 289.

SCRIPTURE *See page 290.*

REFLECTION

Am I living my dream?

PRAYER

Thank you, Giver of Life,
for blessing your creation on earth
with St. Joseph, worker
and foster father to the Son of God.

CANTICLE Canticle of Mary

Morning Prayer

Begin with page 288.

SCRIPTURE John 14:6b

...I am the way and the truth and the life.

BREATHING AND PRAYING

Some deep breathing exercises can enhance both your prayer life and your energy level. Here is a simple exercise to practice while praying.

Stand straight at an open window (if it is cold, crack the window just enough to get some fresh air). With your hands folded together in a prayer posture, begin your prayer by opening your mouth partially and inhaling air from the bottom of your stomach. You will know if you are doing it correctly when you make a rasping sound at the back of your throat. You can both hear and feel the air at the back of your throat. Inhale slowly, bringing your arms up in a praise gesture (raised and apart), saying:

I am the way and the truth...

Hold your arms open for just a second. Then, exhaling slowly, bring your hands down and together in a prayer posture, saying:

...and the life.

Practice this deep breathing prayer method no more than ten times each day. As you say it, you awaken the Christ-consciousness within you. A nice way to end the exercise is to say:

Lord, I consecrate this day to you.

CANTICLE Wisdom Canticle

Evening Prayer

Begin with page 289.

SCRIPTURE John 14:6b

...I am the way and the truth and the life.

REFLECTION

What will happen in my life as I wake up the Christ-consciousness within me?

PRAYER

Practice the exercise two or three times.

CANTICLE Canticle of Mary

Morning Prayer

Begin with page 288.

SCRIPTURE John 6:68-70a

Simon Peter answered him, "Master, to whom shall we
go? You have the words of eternal life. We have come to
believe and are convinced that you are the Holy One of
God." Jesus answered them, "Did I not choose you
twelve?"

MEDITATION

Why is it so important for humankind to hear the word of
"eternal life"? Why do we seek eternity? Why can't we be
fulfilled in our temporary, present state? Maybe part of
the answer is that until we lose our physical limitations,
we are not free to become what we were created for. Just
what were we created for? Meditate on your answer to
that question.

SILENT MEDITATION

PRAYER

Purify my thoughts, Lord.
Charge my actions with divine inspiration
and channel my love to selfless service.

CANTICLE Canticle of St. Patrick

Evening Prayer

Begin with page 289.

SCRIPTURE John 6:68c

You have the words of eternal life.

REFLECTION

What am I doing to live a life in the Spirit—to be as free as I can of earthly limitations?

PRAYER

My soul waits with eagerness
to soar to you,
divine Spirit and merciful Master.
In sleep, I now relax in the God of Love.

CANTICLE Canticle of St. Francis

Morning Prayer

Begin with page 288.

SCRIPTURE Matthew 6:24

No one can serve two masters. He will either hate one and love the other, or be devoted to one and despise the other. You cannot serve God and mammon.

WORDS OF WISDOM

If I could encourage you toward one spiritual discipline, it would be silence and solitude. Feel what you are really feeling; think what you are really thinking. (Richard Rohr, O.F.M.)[1]

PRAYER

Nothing can keep me from you,
Creator God,
except my own ego.

CANTICLE Canticle of Zechariah

Evening Prayer

Begin with page 289.

SCRIPTURE Matthew 6:24c

You cannot serve God and mammon.

REFLECTION

In what ways am I substituting power, prestige and possessions to numb myself from feeling and thinking?

PRAYER

You invite me, Brother Jesus,
to lean on you
rather than on the things of this world.
Thank you for giving me something to hold fast
when I need to let go of my illusions.

CANTICLE Wisdom Canticle

Morning Prayer

Begin with page 288.

SCRIPTURE Isaiah 66:22-23

> As the new heavens and the new earth
>   which I will make
> Shall endure before me, says the LORD,
>   so shall your race and your name endure.
> From one new moon to another,
>   and from one sabbath to another,
> All mankind shall come to worship
>   before me; says the LORD.

PUTTING PRAYER INTO PRACTICE

Be glad for something new—a change of plan, a surprise, even a change that is painful. For it is in this newness that growth occurs.

PRAYER

> Into your depths
> O darkness, draw me that I might lose myself
> in that ultimate void
> where there is neither day nor night
> but suspension of all time,
> there to be transformed—
> caught up in communion
> with the divine presence—
> whence I will emerge anew.

CANTICLE Canticle of St. Francis

Evening Prayer

Begin with page 289.

SCRIPTURE *See page 298.*

REFLECTION

In what ways am I growing? Do I welcome change?

PRAYER

O my Soul! Praise God the Creator!
Sing the song of earth,
dance on the sand
to the sounds of the sea.
Rejoice in the glorious
breath of spring!

CANTICLE Canticle of Judith

Morning Prayer

Begin with page 288.

SCRIPTURE Psalm 66:4-5

"Let all on earth worship and sing praise to you,
   sing praise to your name!"

Come and see the works of God,
   his tremendous deeds among men.

PUTTING PRAYER INTO PRACTICE

In how many ways do we interfere with the joyful sounds
of the earth? The earth is being ravished of its resources.
Do something for the planet today: Recycle your glass,
start using a biodegradable detergent, write to your
congressional representative in support of
environmental legislation.

PRAYER

Among the joyful sounds of the earth are:

the whisper of the wind
   as it travels through a forest of pine,

the yelp of a monkey
   in the Brazilian rain forest,

the sigh of dry land as it absorbs
   the downfall of a soft, summer rain.

Creator God, we give thanks for these joyful sounds!

CANTICLE Canticle of St. Francis

Evening Prayer

Begin with page 289.

SCRIPTURE *See page 300.*

REFLECTION

In what ways do I take for granted the beautiful earth that God has created? How can I be a better steward of God's gifts?

PRAYER

Let me give praise daily
for the wonder of rain,
the glory of trees
and the magnificence of sunsets.
Thank you for surrounding me
with the majesty of your creation,
Creator God.

CANTICLE Canticle of Judith

Morning Prayer

Begin with page 288.

SCRIPTURE John 10:1-5

Amen, Amen, I say to you, whoever does not enter a
sheepfold through the gate but climbs over elsewhere is
a thief and a robber. But whoever enters through the
gate is the shepherd of the sheep. The gatekeeper opens
it for him, and the sheep hear his voice, as he calls his
own sheep by name and leads them out. When he has
driven out all his own, he walks ahead of them, and the
sheep follow him, because they recognize his voice. But
they will not follow a stranger; they will run away from
him, because they do not recognize the voice of
strangers.

PUTTING PRAYER INTO PRACTICE

The wild animals that might break into the sheepfold and
wound or kill the sheep (us) are our fears, uncontrollable
desires and consuming selfishness. Christ, if we allow
him, will be our guard and shepherd. Without the help of
a divine guide, however, we are in danger of being
devoured by our own or another's wild side.

Be aware today of the people, places and situations that
you allow into your life. Are you listening to the
shepherd when you make choices about friends,
business ethics, places of entertainment, etc.?

PRAYER

> You are the Gatekeeper,
> shielding me from negative and destructive forces,
> protecting me from danger.
> At times, in my humanness,
> I will dismiss you from my life
> in my zeal for freedom and self-will.
> But stay near me, Christ,
> even when I stray.
> Find me and bring me back
> to the bosom of your love.

CANTICLE Canticle of St. Patrick

Evening Prayer

Begin with page 289.

SCRIPTURE *See page 302.*

REFLECTION

Do I recognize Christ's voice?

PRAYER Psalm 23:1

The LORD is my shepherd; I shall not want.

CANTICLE Canticle of Zechariah

Opening Song for Morning Prayer

SALUTATION

Morning is a rosebud,
and the day is its bloom.

SONG Psalm 57:8-12

My heart is steadfast, O God; my heart is steadfast;
    I will sing and chant praise.
Awake, O my soul; awake, lyre and harp!
    I will wake the dawn.
I will give thanks to you among the peoples, O Lord,
    I will chant your praise among the nations,
For your kindness towers to the heavens,
    and your faithfulness to the skies.
    Be exalted above the heavens, O God;
      above all the earth be your glory!

Turn to the page with today's date for the continuation of Morning Prayer.

Opening Song for Evening Prayer

SALUTATION

Come, darkness!
Let me devour your void
until daybreak.

SONG Psalm 61:1-4

Hear, O God, my cry;
   listen to my prayer!
From the earth's end I call to you
   as my heart grows faint.
You will set me high upon a rock; you will give me rest,
   for you are my refuge,
      a tower of strength against the enemy.

Turn to the page with today's date for the continuation of Evening Prayer.

Morning Prayer

Begin with page 304.

SCRIPTURE John 10:11b-13

A good shepherd lays down his life for the sheep. A hired man, who is not a shepherd and whose sheep are not his own, sees a wolf coming and leaves the sheep and runs away, and the wolf catches and scatters them. This is because he works for pay and has no concern for the sheep.

PUTTING PRAYER INTO PRACTICE

Give this Scripture some thought today as you move about your workplace, whether it be the market or the home. Are you working for reward—money, status, a place in heaven—or do you own your responsibilities and treat coworkers, customers, superiors or those under your authority as your brothers and sisters?

PRAYER

To follow you, Christ,
it is not necessary
to run off to the missions,
but only to bring your love and service
into the marketplace and the home.

CANTICLE Canticle of St. Patrick

Evening Prayer

Begin with page 305.

SCRIPTURE John 10:13

This is because he works for pay and has no concern for the sheep.

REFLECTION

Who am I concerned about? How and with whom do I spend my time?

PRAYER

You laid down your life
for me.
Your protection is ever-present.
I embrace your essence.

Glory be to the Father....

CANTICLE Canticle of Zechariah

Morning Prayer

Begin with page 304.

SCRIPTURE John 12:46-47

I came into the world as light, so that everyone who believes in me might not remain in darkness. And if anyone hears my words and does not observe them, I do not condemn him, for I did not come to condemn the world but to save the world.

PUTTING PRAYER INTO PRACTICE

Today, as you interact with people, strive to show the merciful side of God (or yourself) rather than the condemning, judgmental side.

PRAYER

Light of the World,
help me to be one small flicker
in your flaming fire of mercy!

CANTICLE Canticle of Mary

Evening Prayer

Begin with page 305.

SCRIPTURE John 12:47c

...I did not come to condemn the world but to save the world.

REFLECTION

How can I use my gifts to reflect the gentle, loving side of God?

PRAYER

Christ, you came to save me
at great sacrifice to yourself.
It is hard for me to grasp such love.

Glory be to the Father....

CANTICLE Canticle of Zechariah

Morning Prayer

Begin with page 304.

SCRIPTURE John 14:1-6a

[Jesus told them,] "Do not let your hearts be troubled.
You have faith in God; have faith also in me. In my
Father's house there are many dwelling places. If there
were not, would I have told you that I am going to
prepare a place for you? And if I go and prepare a place
for you, I will come back again and take you to myself, so
that where I am you also may be. Where [I] am going
you know the way." Thomas said to him, "Master, we do
not know where you are going; how can we know the
way?" Jesus said to him, "I am the way and the truth and
the life."

MEDITATION

Christ is not just talking to his disciples. He is talking to
you. He has prepared a place for you. Meditate now on
this knowledge. Let its meaning sink into your heart.
God has a place prepared for you.

Silence

PRAYER

How wonderful to belong—
to be part of the divine plan.
As you have prepared a place for me,
Brother Jesus,
so I prepare a place for you
in my heart.

CANTICLE Canticle of Judith

Evening Prayer

Begin with page 305.

SCRIPTURE John 14:2c

...I am going to prepare a place for you.

REFLECTION

God, my Father, has reserved a place for me in his
house. How does this speak to me?

PRAYER

I am an undeserving child.
I rest in your mercy and love.
I give thanks to you, Father God.

Glory be to the Father....

CANTICLE Canticle of St. Francis

Morning Prayer

Begin with page 304.

SCRIPTURE John 13:16-17

Amen, amen, I say to you, no slave is greater than his
master nor any messenger greater than the one who sent
him. If you understand this, blessed are you if you do it.

PUTTING PRAYER INTO PRACTICE

Blessed are you who, following the Master's example,
seek to serve rather than be served. Become aware today
of how many times you seek to serve others and how
many times you seek to satisfy your own needs.

PRAYER

Blessed are those
who work for justice
so that every family has
  a house,
  steady work,
  food for the body
  and joy for the soul.
Blessed am I
when I serve humankind in this way.

CANTICLE Canticle of St. Patrick

Evening Prayer

Begin with page 305.

SCRIPTURE *See page 312.*

REFLECTION

Christ tells me I am blessed only when I "do" service. Understanding and believing are not enough. How did I put my faith into action today?

PRAYER

Each day my basic needs are met.
I have more than enough.
I live in freedom without fear.
My joy is complete in you, Lord.

CANTICLE Canticle of Mary

Morning Prayer

Begin with page 304.

SCRIPTURE John 14:16-18

And I will ask the Father, and he will give you another Advocate to be with you always, the Spirit of truth, which the world cannot accept, because it neither sees nor knows it. But you know it, because it remains with you, and will be in you. I will not leave you orphans; I will come to you.

PUTTING PRAYER INTO PRACTICE

The Spirit of truth is always present in the world. God has not abandoned us. But have we abandoned God? Take the time today to find out some truth about a complicated issue—the environment, energy resources, human rights—and how it affects world politics.

PRAYER

Wonderful Counselor,
I wonder how often
history has to repeat itself
merely because we are all consumed
with only the tasks in front of us.

CANTICLE Wisdom Canticle

Evening Prayer

Begin with page 305.

SCRIPTURE *See page 314.*

REFLECTION

Do I know the Spirit of truth? Do I fashion my life and my decisions—especially those decisions involving where I spend my time and money—around the Spirit of truth?

PRAYER

In my darkest hour, Christ,
you do not abandon me.
Instead, you wait, even come after me.
I am not deserving of such love.

CANTICLE Canticle of Zechariah

Morning Prayer

Begin with page 304.

SCRIPTURE John 14:23b

Whoever loves me will keep my word, and my Father will love him, and we will come to him and make our dwelling with him.

BREATHING PRAYER

If you love God, the God of love will come to you and dwell within you. Make this Scripture passage into a breathing prayer for yourself.

As you inhale say:

O God, come.

As you exhale say:

Dwell in me.

PUTTING PRAYER INTO PRACTICE

Repeat this Scripture passage or prayer (or both) to yourself throughout the day. Keep reminding yourself to invite Christ and his Father to dwell within you.

PRAYER

In the silence and stillness of the morning, repeat the above breathing prayer several times.

CANTICLE Canticle of St. Patrick

Evening Prayer

Begin with page 305.

SCRIPTURE *See page 316.*

REFLECTION

In what ways did I invite Christ into my heart today?

Enter your reflections in your spiritual journal, if you are keeping one.

PRAYER

Thank you,
Father God and Brother Jesus,
for making your dwelling
within me.

CANTICLE Canticle of Mary

Morning Prayer

Begin with page 304.

SCRIPTURE John 14:25-27

I have told you this while I am with you. The Advocate, the holy Spirit that the Father will send in my name—he will teach you everything and remind you of all that [I] told you. Peace I leave with you; my peace I give to you. Not as the world gives do I give it to you. Do not let your hearts be troubled or afraid.

PUTTING PRAYER INTO PRACTICE

Being passive is not being peaceful. Working for peace requires the stamina of a soldier. If we are neutral or silent about discrimination or injustice, then we play into the hands of the oppressor. Neutrality never helps the victim, only the villain. Let your actions today reveal whose side you are on.

PRAYER

I'd prefer to be silent, Lord,
to remain anonymous,
rather than endure the rebuke
of my fellow humans
when I take a stand against injustice.
Give me the courage, God,
to face the battle for peace.

CANTICLE Canticle of Zechariah

Evening Prayer

Begin with page 305.

SCRIPTURE John 14:27ab

> Peace I leave with you; my peace I give to you. Not as the world gives do I give it to you.

REFLECTION

> In what ways do my actions reflect care and concern for the vulnerable and weak?

Enter your reflections in your spiritual journal, if you are keeping one.

PRAYER

> You show us the beauty of brotherhood, Jesus,
> and the joys of caring.
> In gratefulness, I greet the peace of sleep.

CANTICLE Canticle of St. Francis

Opening Song for Morning Prayer

SALUTATION

O sun,
steadfast and glowing,
you are a symbol
of divine love!

SONG Psalm 34:2-4

I will bless the LORD at all times;
   his praise shall be ever in my mouth.
Let my soul glory in the LORD;
   the lowly will hear me and be glad.
Glorify the LORD with me,
   let us together extol his name.

Turn to the page with today's date for the continuation of Morning Prayer.

Opening Song for Evening Prayer

SALUTATION

Fill me with your peace, Lord,
as the day departs and darkness descends.

SONG Psalm 34:5-10

I sought the LORD, and he answered me,
and delivered me from all my fears.
Look to him that you may be radiant with joy,
and your faces may not blush with shame.
When the afflicted man called out, the LORD heard,
and from his distress he saved him.
The angel of the LORD encamps
around those who fear him, and delivers them.
Taste and see how good the LORD is;
happy the man who takes refuge in him.
Fear the LORD, you his holy ones,
for nought is lacking to those who fear him.

Turn to the page with today's date for the continuation of Evening Prayer.

Morning Prayer

Begin with page 320.

SCRIPTURE Matthew 6:6a

But when you pray, go to your inner room, close the door, and pray to your Father in secret.

WORDS OF WISDOM

The shadow is all those things we want to get behind us and walk away from—the part of me I really don't feel good about, the part of me I would like to throw away, the part of me I do not want anyone else to see.

We can come to recognize the shadow's presence by answering these questions: What do I rarely talk about with others? When do I get sensitive or touchy? When do I feel inferior? What positives/negatives do people point out to me that I have difficulty accepting? (Richard J. Sweeney, Ph.D.)[2]

PRAYER

I go into my room
to pray in secret
and to face that part of me
I have disowned.
Help me, Lord, to love
and bring to light
the "enemy within."

CANTICLE Canticle of Zechariah

Evening Prayer

Begin with page 321.

SCRIPTURE Matthew 6:6a

> But when you pray, go to your inner room, close the door, and pray to your Father in secret.

REFLECTION

> What part of myself am I hiding? When do I feel the most dissatisfied?

Enter your reflections in your spiritual journal, if you are keeping one.

PRAYER

> You bring light to my shadow
> and understanding to my shame.
> In you, I am made whole.

CANTICLE Canticle of Mary

Morning Prayer

Begin with page 320.

SCRIPTURE John 15:1

I am the true vine, and my Father is the vine grower.

UNDERSTANDING THE STAGES OF MORAL DEVELOPMENT

For the next six days Kohlberg's stages of moral development will be explored. Lawrence Kohlberg was an educator and psychologist who did much research in the moral development of children and adults. He concluded that individuals solved moral dilemmas at six different levels. The more one understands and recognizes these stages, the more tolerant and open one is to another's viewpoint.

The focus of the individual on the first level of development is to obey authority and avoid punishment. Morality is seen as external—something big people or authorities say one must do. For example, people at this level would say that stealing is bad because of the punishment involved.

Notice today when you or those around you (especially children) respond to moral dilemmas in this fashion.

PRAYER

You are the source of life,
Creator God,
the root of my existence.

CANTICLE Canticle of St. Patrick

Evening Prayer

Begin with page 321.

SCRIPTURE *See page 324.*

REFLECTION When and why am I obedient to God's word?

PRAYER

>I am the seed of your creation;
>you are the gardener of my soul.
>In thankfulness and praise,
>I rest in your loving hands.

CANTICLE Canticle of St. Francis

Morning Prayer

Begin with page 320.

SCRIPTURE John 15:4

Remain in me, as I remain in you. Just as a branch cannot bear fruit on its own unless it remains on the vine, so neither can you unless you remain in me.

UNDERSTANDING THE STAGES OF MORAL DEVELOPMENT

At the second stage the individual recognizes that there is more than one right view. What is right is what serves the person's own best self-interest. A sense of fair play develops at this level—I'll do something for you if you do something for me. The individual on this level sees the self only as an individual, not as a member of society. Therefore, it is all right to steal from someone who is charging too much or is unwilling to make a fair deal. Since everything is relative, each person is free to pursue his or her own individual interests.

See how many times today you make decisions based on your own individual interests.

PRAYER

Christ the vine,
let me remain in you—
not out of self-interest alone,
but out of love and reverence
for the entire garden of life.

CANTICLE Canticle of St. Francis

Evening Prayer

Begin with page 321.

SCRIPTURE *See page 326.*

REFLECTION

In what ways did I pursue my own self-interest today?

PRAYER

There is no distance
between the vine and the branch.
On the contrary
they are intermingled,
sometimes indistinguishable.
Protect me, Lord,
when I shoot off on my own;
nourish me, although I'm often consumed
with self-interest.

CANTICLE Wisdom Canticle

Morning Prayer

Begin with page 320.

SCRIPTURE John 15:5

I am the vine, you are the branches. Whoever remains in me and I in him will bear much fruit, because without me you can do nothing.

UNDERSTANDING THE STAGES OF MORAL DEVELOPMENT

At the third stage, interpersonal relationships are the key. Good behavior means having good motives and feelings, such as love, empathy, trust and concern for others. This works best in two-person relationships or with family members.

Someone functioning at this level would steal medicine to save his wife's life.

Pay attention to your intimate relationships today and notice the times you make choices based on your concern for another's well-being.

PRAYER

Striving for growth,
I grasp at goodness
only to realize
that to grip the divine
is to let go.

Glory be to the Father....

CANTICLE Canticle of Mary

Evening Prayer

Begin with page 321.

SCRIPTURE *See page 328.*

REFLECTION

At what times today was I motivated by my concern for a loved one?

PRAYER

Lover, Teacher, Christos!
You grace us with your goodness.

CANTICLE Canticle of Zechariah

Morning Prayer

Begin with page 320.

SCRIPTURE John 15:9-10

As the Father loves me, so I also love you. Remain in my love. If you keep my commandments, you will remain in my love, just as I have kept my Father's commandments and remain in his love.

UNDERSTANDING THE STAGES OF MORAL DEVELOPMENT

Those at stage four are concerned with society as a whole. Obeying laws and performing duties is important so that the social order is maintained. People on this level respect authority not because they fear punishment (as in stage one), but because they understand that law and order are good for society. No one at this level would think of breaking a law—even a bad law.

Listen to the people who criticize people who protest for peace, civil rights, pro-life issues. Chances are they are at this stage.

PRAYER

Your commandments, God,
show us how to share
your kingdom here on earth
with each other.

CANTICLE Canticle of Zechariah

Evening Prayer

Begin with page 321.

SCRIPTURE *See page 330.*

REFLECTION

To whom and to what do I give authority over me?

PRAYER

I am grateful for your guidelines,
wise and knowing God,
for they lead me to happiness.

CANTICLE Wisdom Canticle

Morning Prayer

Begin with page 320.

SCRIPTURE John 14:30-31ab

> I will no longer speak much with you, for the ruler of the world is coming. He has no power over me, but the world must know that I love the Father and that I do just as the Father has commanded me.

UNDERSTANDING THE STAGES OF MORAL DEVELOPMENT

At stage four, people want to keep society functioning. A smoothly functioning society, however, is not necessarily a good one. A totalitarian society may be well-organized, but it is hardly the moral ideal. At stage five, people begin to ask, "What makes for a good society?" They believe that a good society is best conceived as a social contract into which people freely enter to work toward the benefit of all.

Stage five subjects, then, talk about "morality" and "rights" that take some priority over particular laws. An independent effort is made to think out what any society ought to value.

PRAYER

Christ our brother,
you are the Lamb of God
and the Shepherd of God's people.
From you we learn to cultivate our conscience.
Give us the wisdom to use it wisely.

CANTICLE Canticle of Judith

Evening Prayer

Begin with page 321.

SCRIPTURE *See page 332.*

REFLECTION

Can I think of some good reasons not to follow a command from my superiors or my boss, or to obey an unjust law?

PRAYER

Quietly, you steal upon me,
divine Spirit,
and nudge the edges of my consciousness
to a higher plane of love.

CANTICLE Wisdom Canticle

Morning Prayer

Begin with page 320.

SCRIPTURE John 16:12-15

I have much more to tell you, but you cannot bear it now. But when he comes, the Spirit of truth, he will guide you to all truth. He will not speak on his own, but he will speak what he hears, and will declare to you the things that are coming. He will glorify me, because he will take from what is mine and declare it to you. Everything that the Father has is mine; for this reason I told you that he will take from what is mine and declare it to you.

UNDERSTANDING THE STAGES OF MORAL DEVELOPMENT

At stage six, the basis for moral reasoning is justice. Democratic processes do not always create just outcomes. The principles of justice require us to treat the claims of all parties in an impartial manner, respecting the basic dignity of all people as individuals. The principles of justice are therefore universal; they apply to all. At this stage, for example, we would not vote for a law that aids some people but seriously hurts others. The principles of justice guide us toward decisions based on an equal respect for all. In actual practice, Kohlberg says, we can reach just decisions by looking at a situation through one another's eyes.

One issue that distinguishes the fifth stage from the sixth is civil disobedience. People at stage five would be more hesitant to endorse civil disobedience because of their commitment to the social contract and to changing laws through democratic agreements. Only when an individual right is clearly at stake does violating the law seem justified. At the sixth stage, in contrast, a commitment to justice makes the rationale for civil disobedience stronger and broader.

PRAYER

The truth is hard to bear, Prince of Peace;
I find comfort in my illusions.
Give me the courage to make choices for justice.

CANTICLE Wisdom Canticle

Evening Prayer

Begin with page 321.

SCRIPTURE *See page 334.*

REFLECTION

Would I choose to send money to children who need food and basic medical attention rather than buy luxury items for myself and my family?

PRAYER

Thank you for your invisible presence.
I stand disposed to do your will.
In you, God, I find my own integrity.

CANTICLE Canticle of Mary

Opening Song for Morning Prayer

SALUTATION

I rejoice in the majesty of the morning
and give glory to you, God, for this day.

SONG Psalm 66:1-4

Shout joyfully to God, all you on earth,
    sing praise to the glory of his name;
    proclaim his glorious praise.
Say to God, "How tremendous are your deeds!
    for your great strength your enemies fawn upon you.
Let all on earth worship and sing praise to you,
    sing praise to your name!"

*Turn to the page with today's date for the continuation of
Morning Prayer.*

Opening Song for Evening Prayer

SALUTATION

I lay my burdens before you, loving God,
letting go of earthly cares and concerns,
and come to you now in prayer and praise.

SONG Psalm 66:16-20

Hear now, all you who fear God, while I declare
  what he has done for me.
When I appealed to him in words,
  praise was on the tip of my tongue.
Were I to cherish wickedness in my heart,
  the LORD would not hear;
But God has heard;
  he has hearkened to the sound of my prayer.
Blessed be God who refused me not
  my prayer or his kindness!

Turn to the page with today's date for the continuation of Evening Prayer.

Morning Prayer

Begin with page 336.

SCRIPTURE 1 John 3:17-18

If someone who has worldly means sees a brother in need and refuses him compassion, how can the love of God remain in him? Children, let us love not in word or speech but in deed and truth.

WORDS OF WISDOM

Christians should willingly and wholeheartedly support the establishment of an international order that includes a genuine respect for legitimate freedom and friendly sentiments of brotherhood towards all men. It is all the more urgent now that the greater part of the world is in a state of such poverty that it is as if Christ himself were crying out in the mouths of these poor people to the charity of his disciples. Let us not be guilty of the scandal of having some nations, most of whose citizens bear the name of Christians, enjoying an abundance of goods, while others lack the necessities of life and are tortured by hunger, disease, and all kinds of misery. For the spirit of poverty and charity is the glory and witness of Christ's Church. (*The Church in the Modern World*)

PRAYER

In the Spirit of love,
I seek justice
and work for peace.

CANTICLE Canticle of Mary

Evening Prayer

Begin with page 337.

SCRIPTURE *See page 338.*

REFLECTION

Do I see how my spirituality can be expressed differently at different levels? Do I also see how Scripture and the Church relate at all the different levels of moral development?

PRAYER

I give thanks for your Church, Christ,
and for all the living examples of spirituality
I find among the people of God.

CANTICLE Canticle of Zechariah

Morning Prayer

Begin with page 336.

SCRIPTURE John 16:7-11

> But I tell you the truth, it is better for you that I go. For if I do not go, the Advocate will not come to you. But if I go, I will send him to you. And when he comes he will convict the world in regard to sin and righteousness and condemnation: sin, because they do not believe in me; righteousness, because I am going to the Father and you will no longer see me; condemnation, because the ruler of this world has been condemned.

PRAYER

> You came to us,
> Brother Jesus,
> as Teacher and Healer.
> You opened our ears
> to the wisdom of the word.
> You gave us light
> to break up our darkness.
> But the Spirit remained outside of us.
> Now enter the Advocate,
> who plants seeds of truth and love
> in our hearts
> so that the risen Christ
> may dwell forever within.

CANTICLE Wisdom Canticle

Evening Prayer

Begin with page 337.

SCRIPTURE *See page 340.*

REFLECTION

Do I sometimes lean on Christ too much, expecting him
to do my work?

PRAYER

Spirit of Truth,
You dwell in my heart.
I welcome your presence
and rest in your care.

CANTICLE Canticle of St. Francis

Morning Prayer

Begin with page 336.

SCRIPTURE John 16:23b-24

Amen, amen, I say to you, whatever you ask the Father in
my name he will give you. Until now you have not asked
anything in my name; ask and you will receive, so that
your joy may be complete.

COMMENTARY

This is one of several places in Scripture where Jesus
tells us that whatever we ask in his name will be given.
"In my name" may mean in the name of the Spirit of love
and truth. Our perception of love and truth is limited, but
the more we seek to understand the Father's kingdom
(as Christ did), the more we walk in his will and the more
we become channels of his divine energy.

PRAYER

Make me an instrument of your peace.
Where there is despair, [let me sow] hope;
Where there is darkness, light;
And where there is sadness, joy.
(Attributed to St. Francis)

CANTICLE Canticle of St. Francis

Evening Prayer

Begin with page 337.

SCRIPTURE *See page 342.*

REFLECTION

In the name of the Son of God or in the name of love, did I ask for anything today?

SUGGESTION

If you are keeping a spiritual journal, keep track of your requests and the spirit in which they were requested. Also keep track of God's response—whenever that occurs.

CANTICLE Canticle of Mary

Morning Prayer

Begin with page 336.

SCRIPTURE John 17:13-16

But now I am coming to you. I speak this in the world so that they may share my joy completely. I gave them your word, and the world hated them, because they do not belong to the world any more than I belong to the world. I do not ask that you take them out of the world but that you keep them from the evil one. They do not belong to the world any more than I belong to the world.

MEDITATION

What does "in the world" mean? Could it be that the natural forces of self-preservation—the big fish eating the little fish—dominate the physical world? Is it only when we reach for our divine nature that we can control and focus our natural animal instincts rather than let them control us?

Meditate on your own perception of what "living in the world" means.

PRAYER

Breaking beyond human nature,
transcending my weakness,
I grasp the divine.

CANTICLE Wisdom Canticle

Evening Prayer

Begin with page 337.

SCRIPTURE John 17:15

I do not ask that you take them out of the world but that you keep them from the evil one.

REFLECTION

Ask Jesus now how you can bring more of the divine into your day-to-day activities. Sit in silence for a few minutes and wait for an answer.

PRAYER

You are the power of love made manifest;
you give me your word
so that I too may overcome the world.

CANTICLE Canticle of Judith

Morning Prayer

Begin with page 336.

SCRIPTURE John 17:17-19

Consecrate them in the truth. Your word is truth. As you
sent me into the world, so I sent them into the world.
And I consecrate myself for them, so that they also may
be consecrated in truth.

PUTTING PRAYER INTO PRACTICE

Truth is like an artichoke. The tough protective outside
leaves must be stripped away before the heart of the
matter can become visible.

Strip yourself today of a prejudice, an opinion or an
attitude that keeps you from seeing the truth.

PRAYER

Lamb of God,
you stood naked
in your tenderness and vulnerability.
Give me the grace of gentleness
and the humility to stand exposed
in my selfishness.

CANTICLE Canticle of Zechariah

Evening Prayer

Begin with page 337.

SCRIPTURE *See page 346.*

REFLECTION

What does it mean to be consecrated in truth? In what ways do I hide my faults from others?

PRAYER

Brother Jesus,
you brought us the truth
and paid the price for its telling.

Lamb of God,
you take away the sins of the world;
have mercy on us.

Lamb of God,
you take away the sins of the world;
grant us peace.

CANTICLE Wisdom Canticle

Morning Prayer

Begin with page 336.

SCRIPTURE John 17:20-22a, 23bc

I pray not only for them, but also for those who will believe in me through their word, so that they may all be one, as you, Father, are in me and I in you, that they also may be in us, that the world may believe that you sent me. And I have given them the glory you gave me...that they may be brought to perfection as one, that the world may know that you sent me, and that you loved them even as you loved me.

COMMENTARY

A few days ago we explored the meaning of "being in the world." Christ came to tell us that there is more to life than the sensory world and that love, not self-preservation, is the driving force of all creation.

PRAYER

Your love exploded
and brought forth creation.
You lifted the lowly,
giving wings to each heart
and claiming paternity
over all souls.

CANTICLE Canticle of Mary

Evening Prayer

Begin with page 337.

SCRIPTURE John 17:23a

I in them and you in me...

REFLECTION

What is my worldview and why am I here?

PRAYER

Our Father, who art in heaven....

CANTICLE Canticle of Zechariah

Morning Prayer

Begin with page 336.

SCRIPTURE Matthew 28:18-20

Then Jesus approached and said to them, "All power in heaven and on earth has been given to me. Go, therefore, and make disciples of all nations, baptizing them in the name of the Father, and of the Son, and of the holy Spirit, teaching them to observe all that I have commanded you. And behold, I am with you always, until the end of the age."

PUTTING PRAYER INTO PRACTICE

How are you responding to your own baptism and its grace for a fuller life? How is your dedication to the Kingdom of Love manifesting itself in your life and in the lives of those around you?

PRAYER

Make me conscious today,
Creator of new life,
of my baptismal commitment.
In the name of God the Father,
Jesus the Son and the Holy Spirit,
I will try to teach, by my actions,
what you have commanded.
And when I stumble and am unsure,
I know even then that you are with me.

Glory be to the Father....

CANTICLE Canticle of St. Patrick

Evening Prayer

Begin with page 337.

SCRIPTURE Matthew 28:20b

And behold, I am with you always, until the end of the age.

REFLECTION

Do I remember, when things are going badly, that God is still with me? In fact, God may be with me more when I stumble than when things are going well.

PRAYER

For your faithful
and unconditional love,
I give thanks.

CANTICLE Canticle of Mary

Morning Prayer

Begin with page 336.

SCRIPTURE John 21:15-17

When they had finished breakfast, Jesus said to Simon
Peter, "Simon, son of John, do you love me more than
these?" He said to him, "Yes, Lord, you know that I love
you." He said to him, "Feed my lambs." He then said to
him a second time, "Simon, son of John, do you love
me?" He said to him, "Yes, Lord, you know that I love
you." He said to him, "Tend my sheep." He said to him
the third time, "Simon, son of John, do you love me?"
Peter was distressed that he had said to him a third time,
"Do you love me?" and he said to him, "Lord you know
everything; you know that I love you." [Jesus] said to
him, "Feed my sheep."

WORDS OF WISDOM

Of what use is it to weigh down Christ's table with
golden cups, when he himself is dying of hunger? First,
fill him when he is hungry; then use the means you have
left to adorn his table. Will you have a golden cup made
but not give a cup of water? What is the use of providing
the table with cloths woven of gold thread, and not
providing Christ himself with the clothes he needs?
What profit is there in that? Tell me: If you were to see
him lacking the necessary food but were to leave him in
that state and merely surround his table with gold, would
he be grateful to you or rather would he not be angry?
What if you were to see him clad in worn-out rags and

stiff from the cold, and were to forget about clothing him and instead were to set up golden columns for him, saying that you were doing it in his honor? Would he not think he was being mocked and greatly insulted? (St. John Chrysostom)[3]

PRAYER/REFLECTION

I was hungry and you gave me directions to a soup kitchen.
I was naked and you offered me thrift store rejects.
I was sick and you asked to see my insurance card.

CANTICLE Canticle of St. Patrick

Evening Prayer

Begin with page 337.

SCRIPTURE AND REFLECTION *See page 352 and above.*

PRAYER

Imagine a world where everyone shared: Starvation and crime would not exist.

Our Father, who art in heaven...

CANTICLE Canticle of Mary

Morning Prayer

Begin with page 336.

SCRIPTURE Luke 1:39-45

During those days Mary set out and traveled to the hill country in haste to a town of Judah, where she entered the house of Zechariah and greeted Elizabeth. When Elizabeth heard Mary's greeting, the infant leaped in her womb, and Elizabeth, filled with the holy Spirit, cried out in a loud voice and said, "Most blessed are you among women and blessed is the fruit of your womb. And how does this happen to me, that the mother of my Lord should come to me? For at the moment the sound of your greeting reached my ears, the infant in my womb leaped for joy. Blessed are you who believed that what was spoken to you by the Lord would be fulfilled."

PRAYER

My soul leaps for joy
at the thought of your presence,
Brother Jesus.

CANTICLE Canticle of Mary

SUGGESTION

Lose yourself in the magnificence of Mary's words. Read the Magnificat again and ponder the phrase that you feel speaks to you.

Evening Prayer

Begin with page 337.

SCRIPTURE Luke 1:53

The hungry he has filled with good things;
the rich he has sent away empty.

REFLECTION

What good things has the Lord filled me with?

PRAYER

For me, too, Lord,
you have done great things.
Generations will not call me blessed,
but in a quiet way you have impregnated me
with the spirit of love
and filled me with good things.
I rejoice and am grateful to you, O God.

CANTICLE Canticle of St. Francis

Morning Prayer

Begin with page 336.

SCRIPTURE 1 John 3:14-16

We know that we have passed from death to life because
we love our brothers. Whoever does not love remains in
death. Everyone who hates his brother is a murderer,
and you know that no murderer has eternal life
remaining in him. The way we came to know love was
that he laid down his life for us; so we ought to lay down
our lives for our brothers.

WORDS OF WISDOM

A sign of human and religious maturity is to integrate the
trauma of death in the context of life. Then death is
dethroned from its status as lord of life and ultimate
reality. Eros [life instincts] triumphs over Thanatos
[death instincts] and desire wins the game. But there is
a price to pay for this immortality: the acceptance of the
mortality of life.

...Those who come to integrate in a complete way the
negative, and especially the trauma of death, certainly
achieve the kingdom of freedom. Nothing will threaten
them anymore.... The kingdom of liberty means, then,
the Kingdom of God. (Leonardo Boff)[4]

PRAYER

> Death does not threaten me.
> It is a doorway to a fuller life,
> free from the boundaries
> of bone and skin.

CANTICLE Canticle of Zechariah

Evening Prayer

Begin with page 337.

SCRIPTURE 1 John 3:14b

> Whoever does not love remains in death.

REFLECTION

> Have I noticed how hate, revenge and resentment drain
> from me the ability to love and enjoy life?

PRAYER

> Love is the eternal essence.
> And you, Christ, are the incarnation of Love.
> I praise and glorify your name.

CANTICLE Canticle of St. Francis

Notes

[1] Excerpt from *Breathing Under Water* by Richard Rohr, O.F.M., copyright ©1989, St. Anthony Messenger Press, is used by permission of St. Anthony Messenger Press.

[2] Excerpt from *You and Your Shadow* by Richard J. Sweeney, copyright ©1988, St. Anthony Messenger Press, used by permission of St. Anthony Messenger Press.

[3] Excerpt from *The Liturgy of the Hours*, copyright ©1974, International Commission on English in the Liturgy, Inc. All rights reserved.

[4] Excerpt from *St. Francis: A Model for Human Liberation*, by Leonardo Boff, English translation copyright ©1982 by The Crossroad Publishing Company, is reprinted by permission of The Crossroad Publishing Company.

June

Opening Song for Morning Prayer

SALUTATION

Ruler of dawn,
you whose touch
ushers in a new day,
energize me with your light
so that I may enter this day
alive in the Spirit.

SONG Psalm 36:6-10

O LORD, your kindness reaches to heaven;
    your faithfulness, to the clouds.
Your justice is like the mountains of God;
    your judgments, like the mighty deep;
    man and beast you save, O LORD.
How precious is your kindness, O God!
    The children of men take refuge in the shadow of your
        wings.
They have their fill of the prime gifts of your house;
    from your delightful stream you give them to drink.
For with you is the fountain of life,
    and in your light we see light.

*Turn to the page with today's date for the continuation of
Morning Prayer.*

Opening Song for Evening Prayer

SALUTATION

Almighty God,
I put aside the concerns of the day
and rejoice in the calm of the night.

SONG Psalm 63:1-8

O God, you are my God whom I seek;
    for you my flesh pines and my soul thirsts
    like the earth, parched, lifeless and without water.
Thus have I gazed toward you in the sanctuary
    to see your power and your glory,
For your kindness is a greater good than life;
    my lips shall glorify you.

Thus will I bless you while I live;
    lifting up my hands, I will call upon your name.
As with the riches of a banquet shall my soul be satisfied,
    and with exultant lips my mouth shall praise you.
I shall remember you upon my couch,
    and through the night-watches I will meditate on you:
That you are my help,
    and in the shadow of your wings I shout for joy.

Turn to the page with today's date for the continuation of Evening Prayer.

Morning Prayer

Begin with page 360.

SCRIPTURE John 21:18-19

[Jesus said,] "Amen, amen, I say to you, when you were younger, you used to dress yourself and go where you wanted; but when you grow old, you will stretch out your hands, and someone else will dress you and lead you where you do not want to go." He said this signifying by what kind of death he would glorify God. And when he had said this, he said to him, "Follow me."

COMMENTARY

Christ's comments to Peter could be a commentary on aging for all of us. When we are young, we are strong, self-directed and in control of what happens to us. As we grow older, we mellow (hopefully) and loosen the reigns of control. If we live to a great age or incur an illness, we rely heavily on others.

PRAYER

My destiny is unknown,
but I will invest in integrity
and inherit the riches
of God's Kingdom.

CANTICLE Canticle of St. Patrick

Evening Prayer

Begin with page 361.

SCRIPTURE John 21:18b

> ...[B]ut when you grow old you will stretch out your hands and someone else will dress you and lead you where you do not want to go.

REFLECTION

What fears do I have of old age?

PRAYER

Wherever there is fear or pain
you say to me, Lord,
"Follow me."
In you, Lord, I place my trust.

CANTICLE Canticle of Zechariah

Morning Prayer

Begin with page 360.

SCRIPTURE 1 Timothy 1:18-19

I entrust this charge to you, Timothy, my child, in
accordance with the prophetic words once spoken about
you. Through them may you fight a good fight by having
faith and a good conscience. Some, by rejecting
conscience, have made a shipwreck of their faith....

WORDS OF WISDOM

A spiritual guide should be silent when discretion
requires and speak when words are of service.
Otherwise he may say what he should not or be silent
when he should speak. Indiscreet speech may lead men
into error and an imprudent silence may leave in error
those who could have been taught. Pastors who lack
foresight hesitate to say openly what is right because
they fear losing the favor of men. As the voice of truth
tells us, such leaders are not zealous pastors who protect
their flocks, rather they are like mercenaries who flee by
taking refuge in silence when the wolf appears.
(St. Gregory the Great.)[1]

PRAYER

Gentle God,
teach me to use my tongue
in good conscience
and to choose my words carefully.

CANTICLE Canticle of St. Patrick

Evening Prayer

Begin with page 361.

SCRIPTURE *See page 364.*

REFLECTION

In what ways today did my words or silence reflect wisdom?

PRAYER

May both my speech and silence
reflect your glory,
Father, Son and Holy Spirit.

CANTICLE Wisdom Canticle

Morning Prayer

Begin with page 360.

SCRIPTURE Sirach 28:1-2

The vengeful will suffer the LORD's vengeance,
for he remembers their sins in detail.

Forgive your neighbor's injustice;
then when you pray, your own sins will be forgiven.

PUTTING PRAYER INTO PRACTICE

Focus on forgiving another's injustice. This is easy to do
if you begin to focus on your own injustices. For
example, pay attention today to the products you
consume. Are their low prices possible because the
workers producing them receive unfair wages?

PRAYER

What good is it, Lord,
to be among the living
if my heart harbors hate?
But how sweet
is the breath of life
to the person who puts on
the yoke of forgiveness.

CANTICLE Canticle of St. Francis

Evening Prayer

Begin with page 361.

SCRIPTURE *See page 366.*

REFLECTION

Did I discover at least one way that I am playing into unjust practices?

PRAYER

You give us the creative power
and sufficient love
to fashion a planet
of plenty for everyone.

Thank you for providing us
with the gifts to build
your kingdom on earth.

Our Father....

CANTICLE Wisdom Canticle

Morning Prayer

Begin with page 360.

SCRIPTURE 2 Corinthians 1:3-5

Blessed be the God and Father of our Lord Jesus Christ, the Father of compassion and God of all encouragement, who encourages us in our every affliction, so that we may be able to encourage those who are in any affliction with the encouragement with which we ourselves are encouraged by God. For as Christ's sufferings overflow to us, so through Christ does our encouragement also overflow.

A STORY

A woman bought a plant that, she was told, produced beautiful blooms. She planted it in her backyard next to a fence. Conscientiously, she tended to it daily, watering and cultivating the ground. It grew to magnificence but no blooms appeared. With all the care and nurturing she was providing, she could not understand why it did not bear flowers.

Then one day the frail elderly neighbor lady who lived on the other side of the fence came over to visit. "You have no idea the amount of enjoyment I get from those beautiful flowers on your plant." Upon hearing these words, the plant-owner looked through the slatted fence and beheld that her plant had spread to the neighbor's side, where it was in full, radiant bloom.

PRAYER

Divine Lover, in joy and eagerness,
I embrace the new day,
ready to renew my love affair with life,
even when results are invisible.

CANTICLE Canticle of Zechariah

Evening Prayer

Begin with page 361.

SCRIPTURE *See page 368.*

REFLECTION

To whom did I bring joy, beauty or comfort today?

PRAYER

Send your healing rays
to my resting heart,
merciful Christ.
Bless and protect me
as I prepare for slumber.

CANTICLE Canticle of Mary

Morning Prayer

Begin with page 360.

SCRIPTURE 1 Corinthians 3:13b-15

It will be revealed with fire, and the fire [itself] will test the quality of each one's work. If the work stands that someone built upon the foundation, that person will receive a wage. But if someone's work is burned up, that one will suffer loss; the person will be saved, but only as through fire.

WORDS OF WISDOM

It is done.

Once again the Fire has penetrated the earth.

Not with the sudden crash of thunderbolt, riving the mountain tops: does the Master break down doors to enter his own home? Without earthquake, or thunderclap: the flame has lit up the whole world from within. All things individually and collectively are penetrated and flooded by it, from the inmost core of the tiniest atom to the mighty sweep of the most universal laws of being: so naturally has it flooded every element, every energy, every connecting link in the unity of our cosmos, that one might suppose the cosmos to have burst spontaneously into flame. (Pierre Teilhard de Chardin, S.J.)[2]

PRAYER

Touch me, Divine Fire,

with the energy of love,
so that your compassion
may become like wildfire.

CANTICLE Canticle of Judith

Evening Prayer

Begin with page 361.

SCRIPTURE *See page 370.*

REFLECTION

Being on fire with the Spirit does not mean being a
workaholic, serving others twenty-four hours a day.
Being on fire with the Spirit often means burning with
the struggle between following one's own will or God's.
Am I alive enough in the Spirit to throw myself into the
heat of this conflict or am I comfortable in my
lukewarmness?

PRAYER

Thank you for the spark of life,
the energy that transforms,
the fire that inspires
and the light that gives vision
to your creation,
God of the Cosmos.

CANTICLE Canticle of Judith

Morning Prayer

Begin with page 360.

SCRIPTURE 2 Peter 1:5-7

For this very reason, make every effort to supplement your faith with virtue, virtue with knowledge, knowledge with self control, self control with endurance, endurance with devotion, devotion with mutual affection, mutual affection with love.

SPIRITUAL EXERCISE

By the Scriptures and through the gift of the Holy Spirit, Christ establishes a community of believers and gives the disciples the wisdom to exhort, teach and chastise. Sit in silence for a few minutes now, welcoming the Holy Spirit into your conscience. Read again Peter's letter (above) and try to discern which "discipline" (of the ones listed) you need to cultivate. After reading the paragraph a few times, one of the disciplines will catch your eye more than the others. Concentrate on how you can grow in that discipline.

Silence

PRAYER

Come, Divine Spirit,
awaken my conscience;
lead me to wholeness,
holy One!

CANTICLE Wisdom Canticle

Evening Prayer

Begin with page 361.

SCRIPTURE *See page 372.*

REFLECTION

Did I sense special direction from the Spirit today?

PRAYER

You breathe new life into me
and into everyone who asks.
Joyful, I sing and dance
to find myself
among the community of believers.

CANTICLE Canticle of Judith

June 7

Morning Prayer

Begin with page 360.

SCRIPTURE 2 Peter 3:13, 17-18

But according to his promise we await new heavens and a new earth in which righteousness dwells....

Therefore, beloved, since you are forewarned, be on your guard not to be led into the error of the unprincipled and to fall from your own stability. But grow in grace and in the knowledge of our Lord and savior Jesus Christ. To him be glory now and to the day of eternity. [Amen.]

PUTTING PRAYER INTO PRACTICE

Could it be that the "new earth" or second coming begins to happen when we let Christ come alive in our hearts?

Let Christ live in your surroundings today by reacting with love to people who annoy you and by building bridges of peace where there is conflict.

PRAYER

In the eyes without light,
in the noise and frenzy
of people chasing after trinkets and pleasure,
you find no hope, Lord,
because greed, rather than love, rules.

CANTICLE Canticle of St. Patrick

Evening Prayer

Begin with page 361.

SCRIPTURE 2 Peter 3:17b

...[B]e on your guard not to be led into the error of the unprincipled and to fall from your own stability.

REFLECTION

At work and in my neighborhood, do I seek to stop gossip and resolve conflict?

PRAYER

I rejoice
in the ways Christ works through me,
and I pray, in gratefulness,
for the ability
to remain rooted in his love.

CANTICLE Canticle of St. Francis

Opening Song for Morning Prayer

SALUTATION

I rise to greet the new day
with a song of love on my lips
for my beloved.

SONG Song of Songs 2:8-10

Hark! my lover—here he comes
    springing across the mountains,
    leaping across the hills.
My lover is like a gazelle
    or a young stag.
Here he stands behind our wall,
    gazing through the windows,
    peering through the lattices.
My lover speaks: he says to me,
    "Arise, my beloved, my beautiful one,
    and come!"

Turn to the page with today's date for the continuation of Morning Prayer.

Opening Song for Evening Prayer

SALUTATION

As the day closes,
help me, Lord,
to find you when I seek you.
Erase the anxiety of the day;
give me your peace
as I prepare for sleep.

SONG Song of Songs 3:1-4a

On my bed at night I sought him
   whom my heart loves—
I sought him but I did not find him.
I will rise then and go about the city;
   in the streets and crossings, I will seek
Him whom my heart loves.
   I sought him but I did not find him.
The watchmen came upon me,
   as they made their rounds of the city:
   Have you seen him whom my heart loves?
I had hardly left them,
   when I found him whom my heart loves.

Turn to the page with today's date for the continuation of Evening Prayer.

Morning Prayer

Begin with page 376.

SCRIPTURE Acts 3:1-7

Now Peter and John were going up to the temple area for
the three o'clock hour of prayer. And a man lame from
birth was carried and placed at the gate of the temple
called "the Beautiful Gate" every day to beg for alms
from the people who entered the temple. When he saw
Peter and John about to go into the temple, he asked for
alms. But Peter looked intently at him, as did John, and
said, "Look at us." He paid attention to them, expecting
to receive something from them. Peter said, "I have
neither silver nor gold, but what I do have I give you: in
the name of Jesus Christ the Nazorean, [rise and] walk."
Then Peter took him by the right hand and raised him
up, and immediately his feet and ankles grew strong.

SPIRITUAL EXERCISE

Sit quietly before the Lord. Let go of all distractions and
worries. Select one person that you would like to please
today. It might be spouse, child, friend, parent, coworker—
even a person you are at odds with. Try to put yourself in
that person's place, thinking and feeling as she or he
does. Then ask the Lord for the light to see what you can
do to please that person.

PRAYER

Bountiful Beloved, may I grow
in awareness of the riches that surround me.

Brother Jesus, as I become a vessel
of your light and love,
help me dare to say, as did Peter,
"I have no silver or gold,
but I give you what I have."

CANTICLE Canticle of Zechariah

Evening Prayer

Begin with page 377.

SCRIPTURE *See page 378.*

REFLECTION

How did I use my gifts today? Did I succeed in pleasing
the one person whom I selected this morning? Did I
open myself up to receive gifts from others?

PRAYER

Thank you, Lord,
for the gifts you have given.

Acknowledge at least three.

Give me the courage, God,
to take responsibility for these gifts
and to use them to serve others.

CANTICLE Canticle of Mary

Morning Prayer

Begin with page 376.

SCRIPTURE Psalm 118:22-23

> The stone which the builders rejected
>   has become the cornerstone.
> By the LORD has this been done;
>   it is wonderful in our eyes.

PUTTING PRAYER INTO PRACTICE

Watch today for people whose standards are rejected by the world. These people can be the building blocks for the Kingdom of love.

PRAYER

It is when I am weak and dejected, Lord,
that you can work wonderful things in me.
For it is at these times that I am most likely
to open up to your grace.

CANTICLE Canticle of Mary

Evening Prayer

Begin with page 377.

SCRIPTURE *See page 380.*

REFLECTION

How does my own fear of rejection sometimes keep me from putting my goodness into action?

PRAYER

You are an enigma, God,
working in the most unlikely people and places.
I am touched and delighted
by your playful presence.

Glory be to the Father....

CANTICLE Canticle of Judith

Morning Prayer

Begin with page 376.

SCRIPTURE Mark 12:17b

Repay to Caesar what belongs to Caesar and to God what
belongs to God.

COMMENTARY

What a clear, crisp statement Jesus gives us on the
distinction between worldly and heavenly obligations.
Each must be paid in its own way!

PRAYER

The world woos me away from you,
Maker of the universe.
Caught up in the created
rather than the Creator,
my priorities get confused.
Grant me the clarity, Divine Spirit, to distinguish
between the Maker and the made.

CANTICLE Wisdom Canticle

Evening Prayer

Begin with page 377.

SCRIPTURE Mark 12:17b

Repay to Caesar what belongs to Caesar and to God what belongs to God.

REFLECTION

What do I owe the world and what do I owe God?

PRAYER

In your debt I stand, God,
giving glory to you,
the initial Investor in the universe.

CANTICLE Canticle of Judith

Morning Prayer

Begin with page 376.

SCRIPTURE Mark 12:32-34ab

> The scribe said to him, "Well said, teacher. You are right in saying, 'He is One and there is no other than he.' And 'to love him with all your heart, with all your understanding, with all your strength, and to love your neighbor as yourself' is worth more than all burnt offerings and sacrifices." And when Jesus saw that [he] answered with understanding, he said to him, "You are not far from the kingdom of God."

PUTTING PRAYER INTO PRACTICE

> Repeat this Scripture passage throughout the day, "You are not far from the kingdom of God" (Mark 12:34b). Remember that whenever you act out of the spirit of love, patience and service, you will not be far from the Kingdom of God.

PRAYER

> As the drama of the universe unfolds,
> do not become discouraged,
> Divine Director,
> when the actors,
> blinded by the worldly stage,
> become unaware of your presence as producer.

CANTICLE Canticle of St. Francis

Evening Prayer

Begin with page 377.

SCRIPTURE Mark 12:34b

You are not far from the kingdom of God.

REFLECTION

At what times today did I feel close to God?

PRAYER

Creator of the Cosmos,
you give me the choice and chance
to build your Kingdom on earth.

Our Father....

CANTICLE Wisdom Canticle

Morning Prayer

Begin with page 376.

SCRIPTURE Matthew 5:13

> You are the salt of the earth. But if salt loses its taste,
> with what can it be seasoned? It is no longer good for
> anything but to be thrown out and trampled underfoot.

PUTTING PRAYER INTO PRACTICE

Salt adds spice and zip! A seasoned Christian does not
play it safe, but makes choices that are fair to everyone
rather than to one particular group. Striving to be fair to
both sides will spice up your life! Try it today and see.

PRAYER

Holy Spirit,
Messenger of Truth and Justice,
may I bring to my business decisions,
a sense of fair play
for both employer and employee.
May I vote for politicians
who will represent all Americans,
not just a select few.
May the choices I make in my parish
be based on the needs
of both sinner and saint.
And may my vision for tomorrow
come from a global perspective
of peace and goodwill
toward all the earth's children.

CANTICLE Canticle of St. Francis

Evening Prayer

Begin with page 377.

SCRIPTURE *See page 386.*

REFLECTION

In what ways am I a bland Christian?

PRAYER

Divine Dove, under your wing,
I receive wisdom and taste truth.
Thank you for seasoning my day with zest.

CANTICLE Wisdom Canticle

Morning Prayer

Begin with page 376.

SCRIPTURE Matthew 5:21-24

You have heard that it was said to your ancestors, "You shall not kill; and whoever kills will be liable to judgment." But I say to you, whoever is angry with his brother will be liable to judgment, and whoever says to his brother, "Raqa" [an Aramaic term of abuse], will be answerable to the Sanhedrin and whoever says, "You fool," will be liable to fiery Gehenna. Therefore, if you bring your gift to the altar, and there recall that your brother has anything against you, leave your gift there at the altar, go first and be reconciled with your brother, and then come and offer your gift.

PUTTING PRAYER INTO PRACTICE

Notice today if you have contempt in your heart for any one person or any group of people.

PRAYER

The fires of Gehenna
are fed by the rage
of resentment and anger.
Shower me, Son of God,
with the cooling rays of your mercy.

CANTICLE Canticle of Zechariah

Evening Prayer

Begin with page 377.

SCRIPTURE Matthew 5:22

But I say to you, whoever is angry with his brother will be liable to judgment, and whoever says to his brother, "Raqa," will be answerable to the Sanhedrin, and whoever says, "You fool," will be liable to fiery Gehenna.

REFLECTION

Am I keeping my distance from someone who has offended me?

PRAYER

My heart sings with the knowledge
that I am forgiven.

CANTICLE Canticle of Mary

Morning Prayer

Begin with page 376.

SCRIPTURE 1 Corinthians 15:45b-49

The first man, Adam, became a living being, the last
Adam a life-giving spirit. But the spiritual was not first;
rather the natural and then the spiritual. The first man
was from the earth, earthly; the second man from
heaven. As was the earthly one, so also are the earthly,
and as is the heavenly one, so also are the heavenly. Just
as we have borne the image of the earthly one, we shall
also bear the image of the heavenly one.

PUTTING PRAYER INTO PRACTICE

Everyone is a wonderful creation of God's handiwork!
Try to remember this today as you look into the eyes of
a brother or sister.

PRAYER

It is difficult, Lord,
to carry the responsibility
that comes with remembering
that I am your work of art.
Teach me humility and self-esteem
as I recognize the miracle of my creation.

CANTICLE Wisdom Canticle

Evening Prayer

Begin with page 377.

SCRIPTURE *See page 390.*

REFLECTION

Did I look on anyone today as a miracle of God's creation? Who? What difference did it make in my relationship with that person? How can I remember to view everyone, including myself, as a miracle?

PRAYER

Thank you, Lord,
for the beauty that surrounds me
within and without.
Almighty Artist,
thank you for making me a masterpiece
in the gallery of the universe.

CANTICLE Canticle of St. Francis

Opening Song for Morning Prayer

SALUTATION

Awake from your slumber, my soul,
and greet the Giver of a new day.

SONG Psalm 19:2-7

The heavens declare the glory of God,
    and the firmament proclaims his handiwork.
Day pours out the word to day,
    and night to night imparts knowledge;
Not a word nor a discourse
    whose voice is not heard;
Through all the earth their voice resounds,
    and to the ends of the world, their message.

He has pitched a tent there for the sun,
    which comes forth like the groom from his bridal
      chamber
    and, like a giant, joyfully runs its course.
At one end of the heavens it comes forth,
    and its course is to their other end;
    nothing escapes its heat.

Turn to the page with today's date for the continuation of Morning Prayer.

Opening Song for Evening Prayer

SALUTATION

How precious is the gift of rest
which comes to those
who trust in the Lord.

SONG Psalm 19:8-10

The law of the LORD is perfect,
   refreshing the soul;
The decree of the LORD is trustworthy,
   giving wisdom to the simple.
The precepts of the LORD are right,
   rejoicing the heart;
The command of the LORD is clear,
   enlightening the eye;
The fear of the LORD is pure,
   enduring forever;
The ordinances of the LORD are true,
   all of them just....

*Turn to the page with today's date for the continuation of
Evening Prayer.*

Morning Prayer

Begin with page 392.

SCRIPTURE 2 Corinthians 12:9b

My grace is sufficient for you, for power is made perfect in weakness.

WORDS OF WISDOM

In the kind of affliction...which can bring either good or ill, we do not know what it is right to pray for; yet, because it is difficult, troublesome and against the grain for us, weak as we are, we do what every human would do, we pray that it may be taken away from us. We owe, however, at least this much in our duty to God: if he does not take it away, we must not imagine that we are being forgotten by him but, because of our loving endurance of evil, must await greater blessings in its place. In this way, *power shines forth more perfectly in weakness.* These words are written to prevent us from having too great an opinion of ourselves if our prayer is granted, when we are impatient in asking for something that it would be better not to receive; and to prevent us from being dejected, and distrustful of God's mercy toward us, if our prayer is not granted, when we ask for something that would bring us greater affliction, or completely ruin us through the corrupting influence of prosperity. In these cases we do not know what it is right to ask for in prayer. (St. Augustine)[3]

PRAYER

> O loving God, I place myself,
> my wants, my needs, my nameless yearnings
> in your hands.

CANTICLE Canticle of Mary

Evening Prayer

Begin with page 393.

SCRIPTURE *See page 394.*

REFLECTION

> In which of my weaknesses can I see God's power
> shining forth?

PRAYER

> Gather me into the force of your love
> and there let me forever remain,
> acting and making choices,
> grounded in the reality of your divine compassion.

CANTICLE Canticle of St. Francis

Morning Prayer

Begin with page 392.

SCRIPTURE Galatians 5:16-18

I say, then: live by the Spirit and you will certainly not gratify the desire of the flesh. For the flesh has desires against the Spirit, and the Spirit against the flesh; these are opposed to each other, so that you may not do what you want. But if you are guided by the Spirit, you are not under the law.

PUTTING PRAYER INTO PRACTICE

Assume that the desires of the flesh are your selfish tendencies and that the desires of the Spirit are your unselfish tendencies. Concentrate now on three of your selfish traits and three of your unselfish traits.

PRAYER

Merciful God,
when I am critical of others,
help me to remember my own selfish tendencies.
When I am critical of myself and feeling discouraged,
help me to remember my unselfish tendencies.

CANTICLE Canticle of Judith

Evening Prayer

Begin with page 393.

SCRIPTURE *See page 396.*

REFLECTION

At what times today was I living in the flesh—motivated by selfish desires? At what times today did I live in the Spirit—motivated by love and concern for others?

PRAYER

For the presence of the Holy Spirit in my life,
for the times I am open and empty enough
to become a vessel of that presence,
I pray in gratitude to you, generous God.

CANTICLE Canticle of Mary

Morning Prayer

Begin with page 392.

SCRIPTURE Matthew 5:39b

> When someone strikes you on (your) right cheek, turn the other one to him as well.

COMMENTARY

This is one of the most misunderstood Scripture passages. Many people interpret meekness as weakness and restraint as passivity. Jesus was in great command of his human nature and able to keep his emotional energies focused on the positive. Again and again he warns us of the cycle of negativity:

> ...[a]nd forgive us our debts
> as we forgive our debtors.... (Matthew 6:12)

> ...[A]ll who take the sword will perish by the sword. (Matthew 26:52b)

> ...[A] person will reap only what he sows.... (Galatians 6:7b)

Anger is part of the negative cycle that gets passed on from person to person and generation to generation.

PRAYER

Centered in your love,
may I absorb the hurt that's hurled my way,
refusing to return it or to pass it on.

CANTICLE Canticle of St. Patrick

Evening Prayer

Begin with page 393.

SCRIPTURE *See page 398.*

REFLECTION

In what way did I stop the cycle of anger today?

PRAYER

As the night approaches,
I rest in peace and comfort
because of your unconditional love, Lord.

CANTICLE Canticle of St. Francis

Morning Prayer

Begin with page 392.

SCRIPTURE Matthew 5:44-45

But I say to you, love your enemies, and pray for those
who persecute you, that you may be children of your
heavenly Father, for he makes his sun rise on the bad
and the good, and causes rain to fall on the just and the
unjust.

PUTTING PRAYER INTO PRACTICE

It is the nature of love to express itself freely without
judgment, without partiality, even without choice. Today
give your attention and kindness to all who come within
your reach.

PRAYER

As shining is the sun's essence,
may loving be mine, Divine Creator.
You who are the source of compassion,
help me freely give
to all who come into my path.
If loving is my nature,
then I must indeed love
the deserving and undeserving alike.

CANTICLE Canticle of St. Francis

Evening Prayer

Begin with page 393.

SCRIPTURE *See page 400.*

REFLECTION

Was there a time today when I could not restrain myself from loving?

PRAYER

Source of love and light,
you give generously
because that is your essence.
How wonderful it is
that the cosmos rests
in your great hands.

CANTICLE Canticle of Mary

Morning Prayer

Begin with page 392.

SCRIPTURE Matthew 6:2a

When you give alms, do not blow a trumpet before you, as the hypocrites do in the synagogues and in the streets to win the praise of others.

PUTTING PRAYER INTO PRACTICE

The word *hypocrite* means "actor." In a sense, everyone puts on a mask and plays roles. Today, strive to be yourself.

PRAYER

Let me begin to dare
to remove my mask of pretense,
confident that I can be loved
just as I am.

CANTICLE Canticle of Mary

Evening Prayer

Begin with page 393.

SCRIPTURE *See page 402.*

REFLECTION

In what way or ways was I truly myself today?

PRAYER

Creator God,
you made me in your image,
and I rejoice
that I was fashioned
after your likeness.

CANTICLE Canticle of Judith

Morning Prayer

Begin with page 392.

SCRIPTURE 2 Corinthians 13:13

The grace of the Lord Jesus Christ and the love of God
and the fellowship of the holy Spirit be with all of you.

PRAYER

Father God, creator of all,
you breathe life into the cosmos
and beauty into being.

Brother Jesus, compassionate counselor,
your divine spark
ignites the tinder of love.

Holy Spirit, formless dimension of truth,
you restore calm and clarity
to consciousness.

Glory be to the Divine Trinity!

Glory be to the Father....

CANTICLE Canticle of Mary

Evening Prayer

Begin with page 393.

SCRIPTURE *See page 404.*

REFLECTION

Which aspect of the Holy Trinity can you most easily relate to: God the Father, creator and protector? Jesus the Son, loving brother and friend? Or the Holy Spirit, source of wisdom and courage?

PRAYER

Read again the Morning Prayer.

CANTICLE Wisdom Canticle

Morning Prayer

Begin with page 392.

SCRIPTURE Matthew 6:19-21

Do not store up for yourselves treasures on earth, where moth and decay destroy, and thieves break in and steal. But store up treasures in heaven, where neither moth nor decay destroys, nor thieves break in and steal. For where your treasure is, there also will your heart be.

PUTTING PRAYER INTO PRACTICE

Watch how you spend your time and to whom or to what you give your attention. That is where your treasure lies.

PRAYER

O Lord, this mortal creature
you fashioned with your hands
needs a few basic things to survive.
Beyond that, let me live simply
and put my efforts into helping those
who are without the basics,
rather than storing a surplus for myself.

CANTICLE Canticle of St. Francis

Evening Prayer

Begin with page 393.

SCRIPTURE Matthew 6:21

For where your treasure is, there also will your heart be.

REFLECTION

How much time do I spend earning money for things I really do not need?

PRAYER

In you, Lord, is my real treasure.
You surround me with beauty and love.
I give praise to your name.

CANTICLE Canticle of Judith

Opening Song for Morning Prayer

SALUTATION

Throughout the day,
may I be attentive to your voice,
Divine Creator,
as it whispers your will.

SONG Psalm 25:1-5

To you I lift up my soul,
    O LORD, my God.
In you I trust; let me not be put to shame,
    let not my enemies exult over me.
No one who waits for you shall be put to shame;
    those shall be put to shame who heedlessly break
        faith.
Your ways, O LORD, make known to me;
    teach me your paths,
Guide me in your truth and teach me,
    for you are God my savior,
        and for you I wait all the day.

Turn to the page with today's date for the continuation of Morning Prayer.

Opening Song for Evening Prayer

SALUTATION

Shadows, silence and solitude
flow like a soothing balm
from the stillness of the night!

SONG Psalm 25:6-10

Remember that your compassion, O LORD,
    and your kindness are from of old.
The sins of my youth and my frailties remember not;
    in your kindness remember me,
    because of your goodness, O LORD.

Good and upright is the LORD;
    thus he shows sinners the way.
He guides the humble to justice,
    he teaches the humble his way.
All the paths of the LORD are kindness and constancy
    toward those who keep his covenant and his decrees.

Turn to the page with today's date for the continuation of Evening Prayer.

Morning Prayer

Begin with page 408.

SCRIPTURE Matthew 7:1-5

Stop judging, that you may not be judged. For as you judge, so will you be judged, and the measure with which you measure will be measured out to you. Why do you notice the splinter in your brother's eye, but do not perceive the wooden beam in your own eye? How can you say to your brother, "Let me remove that splinter from your eye," while the wooden beam is in your eye? You hypocrite, remove the wooden beam from your eye first; then you will see clearly to remove the splinter from your brother's eye.

WORDS OF WISDOM

You don't have to be a sage or a prophet to point out the fact that the twentieth century, which should have been the greatest triumph of civilization of all time—the triumph of science, technology, consumerism—has been the most murderous century in all of history. More people were killed by each other—20 million in the first big war and I think 40 or 50 million killed in the second—than from all other causes since then. It's an interesting paradox for a writer to think about. (Walker Percy)[4]

PRAYER

> Like a child, Lord
> I become angry at times,
> accusing and blaming another,
> failing to see my own selfishness.
> For inner vision, I pray.
> Lord, hear my prayer.

CANTICLE Canticle of Mary

Evening Prayer

Begin with page 409.

SCRIPTURE *See page 410.*

REFLECTION

> Was I able to stop myself today when I wanted to blame
> or criticize?

PRAYER

> You, God, inspire me to noble heights
> and show me the emptiness of hate.
> I rejoice in your wisdom
> and divine instruction.

CANTICLE Wisdom Canticle

Morning Prayer

Begin with page 408.

SCRIPTURE Matthew 7:6

Do not give what is holy to dogs, or throw your pearls before swine, lest they trample them underfoot, and turn and tear you to pieces.

PUTTING PRAYER INTO PRACTICE

Be careful not to sell or prostitute your values for the sake of being popular or gaining material wealth.

PRAYER

Today let me walk in the divine Godhead,
ever conscious of my privileged position
as heir to the kingdom.

CANTICLE Canticle of St. Patrick

Evening Prayer

Begin with page 409.

SCRIPTURE *See page 412.*

REFLECTION

At what times today did I overcome the temptation to do something I would not have been proud of?

PRAYER

Father, Son and Holy Spirit,
I find equilibrium in your being.
You are the source of my happiness.

Glory be to the Father....

CANTICLE Canticle of Mary

Morning Prayer

Begin with page 408.

SCRIPTURE Matthew 7:7-8

Ask and it will be given to you; seek and you will find; knock and the door will be opened to you. For everyone who asks, receives; and the one who seeks, finds; and to the one who knocks, the door will be opened.

PUTTING PRAYER INTO PRACTICE

Ask God today for a spiritual gift—something that will make you a better person. Then, do what you can to be a good steward of that gift.

PRAYER

In confidence, now,
I enter relationships,
trusting myself and the other
to develop the grace to give.

CANTICLE Canticle of Judith

Evening Prayer

Begin with page 409.

SCRIPTURE Matthew 7:7a

Ask and it will be given to you.

REFLECTION

What virtues and graces do I fail to ask for?

PRAYER

Caught up in the tinsel of worldly toys,
I fail to ask for the true treasures
you are ready to bestow upon me,
gracious and generous God.

CANTICLE Canticle of St. Francis

Morning Prayer

Begin with page 408.

SCRIPTURE Matthew 7:13-14

Enter through the narrow gate; for the gate is wide and
the road broad that leads to destruction, and those who
enter through it are many. How narrow the gate and
constricted the road that leads to life. And those who find
it are few.

PRAYER/POEM

Do not be afraid to leave the pavement where the mob
moves. I will be around that unknown bend on the path
less traveled.

Take time away from the crowd. Even though I'm
everyplace, including the heavily traveled routes, you
won't notice me there because you'll have the fellowship
of one another.

Depart from the expressways with their well-marked
signs, secure fences and smooth, graded shoulders. Give
me your fears and insecurities. I will fashion you into a
vessel of my own making and fill you with your own
uniqueness. But I can do this only if you come to me on
the path less traveled.[5]

CANTICLE Canticle of Zechariah

Evening Prayer

Begin with page 409.

SCRIPTURE *See page 416.*

REFLECTION

How many times do I choose the most comfortable route or the line of least resistance?

PRAYER

You give us the courage to chart a new course.

Glory be to the Father....

CANTICLE Wisdom Canticle

Morning Prayer

Begin with page 408.

SCRIPTURE Matthew 7:17

Just so, every good tree bears good fruit, and a rotten tree bears bad fruit.

CONTEMPLATION

The hardest act in the world is to stop one's thoughts and let go of self. Yet this is the very act that liberates the individual and allows one to bear good fruit.
Contemplative prayer is to the pray-er as Everest is to the mountain climber.

PRAYER

To help you in your contemplative prayer, begin by evoking divine aid:

God, I seek to lose myself in prayer.
Surround me with angels, especially my divine guardian.
Protect me from negative and destructive influences
and welcome me into the ether of your holy
consciousness.
In the name of your Son, Jesus, I ask communion
with you, unworthy though I am. Amen.

Now say your breath prayer or centering prayer over and over, staying focused on the words and their meaning. Then, let go of even the breath or centering prayer and remain suspended in union with the Creator. You will know the time to let go—the Spirit will lead you and you will feel airborne. This "union" may last only a few seconds at first. Come out of contemplation with your own prayer of thanksgiving or an Our Father.

Remember that this type of prayer is a gift from the Spirit. For the last several months of daily prayer, you have been growing in the disciplines needed to receive this gift. Contemplative prayer requires practice and fidelity to a prayerful way of life. It is not easy, but it is the true treasure of the spiritual seeker. You have only to look at the lives of the saints to see what wonders are wrought from divine union.

SILENT CONTEMPLATION

Evening Prayer

Begin with page 409.

SCRIPTURE *See page 418.*

PRAYER

Creator God,
only you can nourish
the fruit of the vine.
In your hands, I will grow whole
and ripen with wisdom.

CANTICLE Canticle of Mary

Morning Prayer

Begin with page 408.

SCRIPTURE Matthew 7:21-23

Not everyone who says to me, "Lord, Lord," will enter
the kingdom of heaven, but only the one who does the
will of my Father in heaven. Many will say to me on that
day, "Lord, Lord, did we not prophesy in your name? Did
we not drive out demons in your name? Did we not do
mighty deeds in your name?" Then, I will declare to them
solemnly, "I never knew you. Depart from me, you
evildoers."

PUTTING PRAYER INTO PRACTICE

Why do we have time to do things over but not the time
to do them right in the first place? In our fast-paced
culture, with its emphasis on instant results, we often
don't take the time to do things well. Watch today for the
things you are not doing well—those tasks that you just
hurry through. Slow down and take the time to give your
best.

PRAYER

To think and act
according to one's highest light
is to be centered in Christ.
Today I will take the time
to do things right.
Today I consecrate to you,
Creator God.

CANTICLE Canticle of St. Patrick

Evening Prayer

Begin with page 409.

SCRIPTURE Matthew 7:21

> Not everyone who says to me, "Lord, Lord," will enter the kingdom of heaven, but only the one who does the will of my Father in heaven.

REFLECTION

> In what ways today did I do my best? How does doing my best make me feel?

Enter your reflections in your spiritual journal, if you are keeping one.

PRAYER

> Your Kingdom surrounds me
> whenever I am in tune with your will, God.
> In all things I behold you.

CANTICLE Canticle of Judith

Morning Prayer

Begin with page 408.

SCRIPTURE Matthew 8:8

> The centurion said in reply, "Lord, I am not worthy to have you enter under my roof; only say the word and my servant will be healed."

PUTTING PRAYER INTO PRACTICE

What a wonderful attitude these words reflect! Before Jesus can use his healing powers, it is necessary for the "seeker" to let go of his or her problem. Today, when you catch yourself worrying over a problem, repeat this Scripture passage to yourself and give the outcome to God by letting go.

PRAYER

> Lord, I am not worthy
> to invite you under my roof
> and into my heart.
> I'm not even sure
> I want to let go enough
> so that you can have your way.
> Help me, your humble servant,
> to turn the reins of my life
> over to you.

CANTICLE Canticle of St. Francis

Evening Prayer

Begin with page 409.

SCRIPTURE *See page 422.*

REFLECTION

What is my experience when I turn a problem over to
God for healing? What is my experience when I hang
onto a problem?

PRAYER

Your healing power
is always at my disposal.
I marvel at your mercy
and give praise with a grateful heart!

CANTICLE Canticle of Mary

Morning Prayer

Begin with page 408.

SCRIPTURE Matthew 10:7-10

As you go, make this proclamation, "The kingdom of heaven is at hand." Cure the sick, raise the dead, cleanse lepers, drive out demons. Without cost you have received; without cost you are to give. Do not take gold or silver or copper for your belts; no sack for the journey, or a second tunic, or sandals, or walking stick. The laborer deserves his keep.

PUTTING PRAYER INTO PRACTICE

The Kingdom of God is at hand whenever you put others at ease. Whenever and wherever you find people in a state of disease, soothe and comfort them.

PRAYER

Putting aside private gain
and self-absorption
I enter the suffering of humanity
to comfort and console
by offering service
and by accepting people just as they are.

CANTICLE Canticle of St. Patrick

Evening Prayer

Begin with page 409.

SCRIPTURE Matthew 10:8b

> Without cost you have received; without cost you are to give.

REFLECTION

> If I labor for the Lord in the fields of love and service, will God provide for my basic needs? How much of my labor is for the Lord and how much, beyond basics, is for my own personal gain?

PRAYER

> Generously, God,
> you have dealt with me.
> Generously, then,
> may I deal with others.

CANTICLE Canticle of St. Francis

Morning Prayer

Begin with page 408.

SCRIPTURE Matthew 10:38

[W]hoever does not take up his cross and follow after me is not worthy of me.

PUTTING PRAYER INTO PRACTICE

Usually one thinks of the cross as a particular burden or trial. Consider also the viewpoint that the cross is the meeting ground between two extremes—heaven and earth, spirituality and practicality, love of God and love of our neighbor. How often, for instance, are people unloving in the name of truth and untruthful in the name of love? Today, try to find the middle ground between the opposites in your life.

PRAYER

It is agonizing at times
to find the balance
between being honest and being loving.
To the sting of truth help me apply
the salve of your compassion,
Giver of all good things.

CANTICLE Canticle of St. Patrick

Evening Prayer

Begin with page 409.

SCRIPTURE *See page 426.*

REFLECTION In what ways did I accept the cross today?

PRAYER

>Brother Jesus,
>you experienced the crucifixion
>in an effort to bring
>the Kingdom of God to earth.
>I am in awe of such love.

CANTICLE Canticle of Zechariah

Notes

[1] Excerpt from *The Liturgy of the Hours*, copyright © 1974, International Commission on English in the Liturgy, Inc. All rights reserved.

[2] Excerpt from *The Hymn of the Universe*, by Pierre Teilhard de Chardin, S.J., copyright © 1965 by Harper & Row, is reprinted with the permission of HarperCollins.

[3] The excerpt from *The Liturgy of the Hours*, copyright © 1974, International Commission on English in the Liturgy, Inc. All rights reserved.

[4] Excerpt from "The Novelist's Freedom," by Walker Percy, *Sojourners*, May 1990, p. 29.

[5] Originally published in *Traveling Together: Prayers for Gatherings*, by Mary Sue Taylor (St. Anthony Messenger Press, 1990).